IMAGES
OF
THE
SPIRIT

IMAGES OF THE SPIRIT

Meredith G. Kline

Wipf and Stock Publishers
EUGENE, OREGON

Wipf and Stock Publishers
199 West 8th Avenue, Suite 3
Eugene, Oregon 97401

Images of the Spirit
By Kline, Meredith G.
Copyright©1980 Kline, Meredith G.
ISBN: 1-57910-205-0
Publication date: January, 1999
Previously published by Baker Book House, 1980.

to the grace of murielangelo

Contents

Preface

Some of the central ideas of this monograph were originally developed in the course of writing another book, still forthcoming. Because they had a special importance of their own and invited treatment beyond what might be given to them in the other work, I wrote them up in the form of two articles, published in *The Westminster Theological Journal*: "Creation in the Image of the Glory-Spirit" (39 [1977]: 250-72) and "Investiture with the Image of God" (40 [1977]: 39-62). Following certain new exegetical paths that came into view in the process of writing those articles led to a third article in the series, "Primal Parousia" (40 [1978]: 245-80). Meanwhile, a fourth study was taking shape as I discovered the story of creation in the image of the Glory-Spirit emerging again in my analysis of the nature of the Old Testament prophets. That study of the prophetic embodiment of the *imago Dei* will be found in the present work as chapter three. By the kind permission of the editors of *The Westminster Theological Journal*, the three articles published there appear here, slightly revised, as chapters one, two, and four.

As it turned out, then, the findings reported in chapter 1 opened up and illuminated further unanticipated areas of exploration. Since the demonstration of such heuristic capability is a fair test of the validity of an interpretative model, the case for the soundness of the general exegesis and thesis offered in chapter 1 rests to a considerable extent on the cumulative force of the confirmatory evidence supplied by the studies in the subsequent chapters.

Among those engaged in biblical exegesis it is a familiar experience to find that one's discoveries were discovered by others long ago— we have simply stumbled upon something that had been lost sight of for a while. How little serious attention has been given for quite

9

a long while to the subject of the cloud-theophany (referred to as "the Spirit" in the title of this book) is evident from the fact that a doctoral dissertation prepared at the Pontifical Biblical Institute (and recently published in the series Analecta Biblica) is allegedly the first extensive monograph ever produced on that subject. And it is a Spanish publication by a Basque Jesuit, J. Luzarraga.[1] His examination of discussions of the theme of the theophanic cloud in early postbiblical times discloses, however, that early interpreters within Judaism, and early Christian writers as well, were already making some of the same key connections as are proposed in the present work between certain of the relevant biblical ideas and texts.[2]

But what is thus lost by way of the supposed originality of one's insights is gained by way of support from antiquity for their substantiality. Besides, it would still appear that there is some breaking of fresh ground in the following pages, especially when it comes to the basic concept of the paradigm function of the theophanic Glory-cloud in the creation of the image of God and to the identification of the major symbolic models employed in Scripture to expound the nature of the divine image in man.

The theme of the *imago Dei* is not presented here in the manner of doctrines in a volume of systematic theology. These are exegetical studies of a biblico-theological character, which, as has been indicated, simply sprouted in unexpected directions in what was for me, at least, a process of discovery. It is hoped, however, that these studies will contribute to the development of the doctrine of the *imago Dei* in

---

1. *Las tradiciones de la nube en la biblia y en el judaismo primitivo* (Rome: Biblical Institute Press, 1973). Curiously, at about the same time, a Th.M. dissertation on the subject of the Spirit and the cloud theophany was prepared by Meredith M. Kline at Westminster Theological Seminary. (On this, see below, chapter one, note 5.) Luzarraga's work came into my hands only a few days ago and I became aware of it belatedly only a few weeks ago through the review-summary of it by Leopold Sabourin, "The Biblical Cloud," *Biblical Theology Bulletin* 4 (1974): 290-311.

2. The general neglect of these ancient exegetical suggestions has perhaps been due in part to the fact that they came at times in contexts informed by hermeneutical approaches of an allegorical or otherwise unacceptable sort. Moreover, the stark supernaturalism of the Shekinah phenomenon scares off the typical modern interpreter. Symptomatic of this, even Luzarraga, impressed though he is with the importance of his subject and concerned to rescue it from oblivion, avoids the question of what literal reality, if any, stood behind the biblical tradition of the miraculous cloud.

systematic theology, first, by adding (in effect) a considerable quantity
of relevant data to the scriptural basis of our thinking on this subject
and, second, by sketching in general outline a way the doctrine might
be restructured so as to fit more squarely on this biblical base.

Overlooked though it has been, the idea of creation in the image of
the Glory-Spirit is, in fact, a foundational and pervasive theme in the
Scriptures. We come upon it in historical narration, symbolic representation in the cultus, didactic exposition, and eschatological expectation. The present work merely suggests selectively something of these
biblical riches. Waiting to be pursued further also is the relationship of
the *imago Dei* to certain other major biblical concepts. Once it is seen
that God the Spirit in his theophanic Presence is the divine paradigm
in the creation of the image of God, a conceptual overlap, if not
synonymity, will be recognized between the *imago Dei* and concepts
like messiahship and the Spirit's filling or baptism of God's people.
And to perceive that it is the same Spirit by whose charismatic enduing
the church is qualified to fulfill the great commission who also, as
Paradigm-Creator of man in the image of God, endowed him to execute the cultural commission, is to possess a vital coherence factor for
working out a unified world-and-life field theory, inclusive of creation
and redemption and, within the area of the redemptive accomplishment
of God's creation designs, comprehensive of both holy and common
vocations.

Over and again in the following chapters, usually at a climactic
point, attention turns to the Book of Revelation. From the way these
studies evolved it will be obvious that I cannot claim that any semblance of a symphonic quality that might be produced by this recur-
rence of the Apocalypse theme is the premeditated product of con-
scious artistry. My constant returning to the Apocalypse is just a
natural by-product of a love for this fascinating capstone of biblical
revelation that goes back to student days.

I want to express my special gratitude to my son, Meredith M.
Kline, and to his wife, Miriam—to Meredith for our continuing con-
versation over the years on the leading ideas of this work and to
Miriam for her kindness in preparing the typescript for the publisher.

Chapter One

The Glory-Spirit and His Human Image

When defining the *imago Dei*, dogmatic theology has traditionally tended to engage in an analysis of what constitutes humanness. But to answer the general question "What is man?" is not the same thing as answering the precise question "What is the image of God?". If our objective is to discern what the biblical idea of the image of God is, it would appear necessary to abandon the traditional dogmatic wineskins, go back to the beginning of Genesis, and start afresh.

In the present chapter we will engage in some exegetical exploration and then outline the approach to the *imago Dei* concept that is suggested by our exegetical findings. A new key element will emerge in the exegetical picture—such will be our claim—the discovery that the theophanic Glory was present at the creation and was the specific divine model or referent in view in the creating of man in the image of God.

The Glory-Spirit at the Creation

After the declaration of the creation of things invisible and visible in the beginning (Gen. 1:1),[1] the biblical record notes conditions in the visible world calling for divine action: the "earth" was in a state of unbounded deep-and-darkness (Gen. 1:2a). Then the presence of the Creator who would make light shine in the darkness and set bounds to

---

1. For the interpretation of "the heavens" of Genesis 1:1 as the invisible heavens and their hosts, see Nehemiah 9:5ff.; (cf. Ps. 103:19f.); Psalm 148:1-4; Colossians 1:16. Note also that as the Genesis 1 account continues, the visible heavens emerge as a derivative of what is called "the earth" in verses 1 and 2.

the waters is affirmed in the remarkable statement: "The Spirit of God was hovering over the face of the waters" (Gen. 1:2b).

The verb used in verse 2b ($m^e rah̬ep̄et̬$) occurs again in the Pentateuch[2] only in Deuteronomy 32:11. There, by the use of this verb, the divine activity in leading Israel through "the waste howling wilderness" (v. 10) on the way to Canaan is likened to that of an eagle hovering protectively over its young, spreading out its wings to support them, and so guiding them on to maturity. In Exodus 19:4 God similarly describes himself as bearing Israel on eagles' wings.

It was actually by means of his Glory-Presence that God thus led his people at the time of the exodus. It was in the pillar of cloud and fire that he went before them in the way and afforded them overshadowing protection.[3] To describe the action of the Glory-cloud by the figure of outspread wings was natural, not simply because of the overshadowing function it performed, but because of the composition of this theophanic cloud. For when prophetic vision penetrates the thick darkness, the cloud is seen to be alive with winged creatures, with cherubim and seraphim. The sound of its coming is, in the prophetic idiom, the sound of their wings.[4]

That Moses in his use of the verb $rh̬p$ in Deuteronomy 32:11 is instituting a comparison between God's presence as Israel's divine aegis in the wilderness and God's presence over creation in Genesis 1:2b is put beyond doubt by the fact that he calls that wilderness a $tōh̬û$ (Deut. 32:10). For this is the word he uses in Genesis 1:2a to describe the state of the earth over which the Spirit hovered at creation, and this noun $tōh̬û$, like the verb $rh̬p$, is used by Moses nowhere else. The comparison drawn in Deuteronomy 32:10f. between the exodus event and the creation is extensively elaborated in the Mosaic historiography. Within the broad parallelism that emerges we find that at the exodus reenactment of creation history the divine pillar of cloud and fire was present, like the Spirit of God at the beginning, to bring light into the

---

2. Elsewhere in the Old Testament, only in Jeremiah 23:9. In the Ugaritic epic of Aqhat it refers to the soaring of an eagle.
3. Cf. Isaiah 63:9.
4. Cf., e.g., Ezekiel 1:24; 10:5. In the symbolic conceptualization of the ancient Near East, sovereign divine glory was depicted by a winged disk, which represented the canopy of heaven with associated phenomena like (storm)-clouds.

darkness (and indeed to regulate the day-night sequence), to divide the waters and make dry land appear in the midst of the deep, and to lead on to the Sabbath in the holy paradise land.

In the light of Moses' own interpretive reuse of the unusual verbal imagery of Genesis 1:2b in Deuteronomy 32:11, the "Spirit of God" in the creation record is surely to be understood as a designation for the theophanic Glory-cloud. There is indeed a considerable amount of biblical data that identify the Glory-cloud as peculiarly a manifestation of the Spirit of God. Here we will cite only a few passages where the functions performed by the Glory-cloud are attributed to the Spirit— Nehemiah 9:19, 20; Isaiah 63:11-14; and Haggai 2:5—and mention the correspondence of the work of the Holy Spirit at Pentecost to the functioning of the Glory-cloud at the exodus and at the erection of the tabernacle.[5]

Reflecting on Genesis 1:2, Psalm 104 envisages the Creator Spirit ($r\hat{u}^a h$) as the one who makes the clouds his chariot and moves on the wings of the wind ($r\hat{u}^a h$), making the winds his angel-messengers and flames his servants (vv. 3f.). When we recognize this theophanic cloud-and-wind form of the Spirit in Genesis 1:2, the literary connections between the original creation record and certain redemptive re-creation narratives become more luminous.[6] The flood episode, like the exodus salvation, is portrayed on an elaborate scale as a re-creation event, and the decisive initiating moment is God's making a wind to move over the earth to subdue the waters (Gen. 8:1). In the exodus re-creation itself, the divine agency in dealing with the waters is denoted as a strong, east wind (Exod. 14:21) and, more poetically, as

---

5. For a more comprehensive account of the evidence, see Meredith M. Kline, "The Holy Spirit as Covenant Witness" (Th.M. dissertation, Westminster Theological Seminary, 1972). Cf. my *The Structure of Biblical Authority* (Grand Rapids: Eerdmans, 1975; hereafter, *SBA*), pp. 201f. J. Luzarraga, *Las tradiciones de la nube en la biblia y en el judaismo primitivo* (Rome: Biblical Institute Press, 1973), pp. 234-45, cites evidence from the early Christian Fathers that they recognized the connection between the Holy Spirit and the cloud.

6. Also explained (as perversions of this feature in a pristine creation revelation) are similar representations in pagan creation traditions. In the *Enuma Elish*, the prelude to Marduk's "creative" structuring of the carcass of Tiamat is his approach in the terrifying glory of wind and storm. And in the similar encounter of Baal with Yamm, the Ugaritic epic parallels the soaring eagle figure of Genesis 1:2 in its use of the imagery of swooping falcons to describe Baal's powerful action.

the breath ($rû^{a}h$) of God's nostrils blown upon the waters (Exod. 15:8, 10).[7]

What Genesis 1:2 identifies as Spirit, Hebrews 1:2, 3 identifies as Son; God is one. Hebrews 1:2b attributes to the Son the creation of the world.[8] Then, before the sustaining, directing role of the Son in divine providence is dealt with in Hebrews 1:3b, he is identified as the image and glory of God, "the effulgence of his glory and the very image (*charaktēr*) of his being" (v. 3a). This description of the likeness of the Son to the Father does not refer to the eternal ontological reality of God apart from creation but to the revelation of the Father by the Son in creation. Reasons for this conclusion are that historical revelation is the theme of this passage (cf. vv. 1, 2a), that the thought has already moved into the sphere of creation at verse 2b, and that the language of verse 3a itself is, of course, that of manifestation. Moreover, the location of this statement between affirmations concerning the Son's role in creation and providence (vv. 2b and 3b) does not favor taking this divine manifestation as a reference to the incarnation. The only way to satisfy the contextual requirements then would seem to be to understand verse 3a in terms of pre-incarnation theophany, and, in particular, the Glory revelation of the Creator spoken of in Genesis 1:2b. The allusion to Genesis 1:2 in verse 3a would then account for the use of the verb "bearing" (*pherō*) in verse 3b.[9]

From the beginning the Son participated in the majesty of the divine Glory so that his royal session on the right hand of God after he had dealt with our sins (Heb. 1:3c and d) was a glorifying of the Son with the glory he had with the Father before the world was[10] and which found its effulgence in the Spirit-Glory at creation. In creating all things, the Word of God who was in the beginning thus proceeded forth from the Spirit of God—as did also the incarnate Word and the

---

7. Cf. also Daniel 7:2; Job 38:1, 4ff.
8. Cf. John 1:3; Colossians 1:16f.
9. In the Septuagint of Genesis 1:2, *epipherō* is used. Cf. Acts 2:2. Recurrent throughout the Book of Hebrews is this theme of the divine Glory bearing the covenant people to the Sabbath-land, to the heavenly Jerusalem on Mount Zion (corresponding to Glory-cloud covered Sinai), into the holy of holies and the awesome presence of their God, a consuming fire.
10. Cf. John 17:5.

inscripturated Word. We are confronted again with this mystery of the Son's identity with the Spirit and his personal distinctiveness and his procession from the Spirit in the figure of that Angel associated with the Glory-cloud and called "the Angel of the Presence" (Isa. 63:9ff.; Exod. 32:2, 12–15).[11]

The Spirit of God hovered over the primeval *tōhû* not only as a creating power but as a paradigm for creation. The theophanic Glory was an archetypal pattern for the cosmos and for man, the image of God. In order to perceive this archetypal working of the Spirit and appreciate its significance for the image-of-God idea, we must have a fairly distinct apprehension of the Bible's representation of the multifaceted phenomenon of the Glory-Spirit that was present at the creation.[12]

When the inner reality veiled within the theophanic cloud is revealed, we behold God in his heaven. The world of the Glory theophany is a dimensional realm normally invisible to man, where God reveals his presence as the King of glory enthroned in the midst of myriads of heavenly beings.[13] It is the realm into which the glorified Christ, disappearing from human view, entered to assume his place on the throne of God. It is the invisible (or "third") heaven brought into cloud-veiled visibility. Thus, the Spirit-Glory of Genesis 1:2b answers to the invisible heavens of Genesis 1:1 and represents a coming forth of the Lord of glory out of invisibility into a special earth oriented and adapted manifestation to create and consummate, to reveal himself in earth history as Alpha and Omega.

God's theophanic glory is the glory of royal majesty. At the center of the heavens within the veil of the Glory-cloud is found a throne; the Glory is preeminently the place of God's enthronement. It is, there-

---

11. Because this Angel was the Son, he enjoyed a name more excellent far than the other angels associated with the theophanic Glory (Heb. 1:4ff.). Significantly, the comparison of Jesus, the image of God's glory, with angels leads to the topic of man as image of God, which also involves comparison with the angels (cf. Heb. 2:6ff.).

12. On this subject see J. Luzarraga, *Las tradiciones*.

13. Ezekiel's visions of the divine Glory (Ezek. 1:1ff.; 3:12ff.; 10:1ff.; 11:22ff.; 43:2ff.) are, of course, a good place to start, but once it is determined that the Glory is a revelational modality of heaven, every biblical unveiling of the scene of the heavenly throne and the divine council becomes a source for our envisaging of the divine presence within the cloud-theophany.

fore, a royal palace, site of the divine council and court of judgment.[14]
As royal house of a divine King, the dwelling of deity, it is a holy
house, a temple. Yet the Glory is not a static structure, but mobile, for
the throne is a chariot-throne, Spirit directed and propelled through the
winged beings, a vehicle of divine judgment, moving with the swift-
ness of light to execute the sentence of the King.

So it was perceived by eyes supernaturally opened and so trans-
cribed in prophetic words. Seen by the natural eye, it was a heavenly
phenomenon of light and clouds. Adapting its form to its function, it
appeared in the varied modes of the sky, now a clear firmament or
sheltering canopy, now a whirlwind or thunderhead of terrifying trumpet and flashing arrow.[15]

The theophanic glory was expressed as light, at whatever dimensional level it was perceived or whatever guise the divine epiphany
assumed in other respects. The appearance of the Glory was the appearance of light as of fire or the sun, the light of divine glory that no
man can approach.[16] This theophanic light appeared at times as a
rainbow radiance expressive of the holy beauty of the Lord in his
temple;[17] at times, as the illuminating light of wisdom and truth, pene-
trating the darkness in the service of judicial righteousness to expose
the works of darkness;[18] and again as an effective energy, executing
judgment whether to bless or curse, whether as a sun of righteousness
rising with healing in its wings or as a light like the blinding, searing
glare of the burning oven.[19]

When most distinctly perceived, the divine figure enthroned in the
Glory is seen as anthropomorphous. The Glory as such is also an-
thropomorphically denoted as the divine face and arm, or hand, or as
parts thereof—eyes and finger. By these terms the Glory is identified
as the personal presence of God and as the power of God stretched

---

14. Cf. I Kings 22:19ff.; Job 1:6; 2:1ff.; Isaiah 6:1ff.; Daniel 7:10; Revelation 4:4.
15. Cf. Exodus 13:21; 14:24; 19:16ff.; 24:10ff.; Psalms 29; 97:2ff.; Job 38:1ff.
16. Cf. I Timothy 6:16.
17. Ezekiel 1:28; Revelation 4:3; 10:1.
18. Daniel 7:9ff.; Psalm 139:7, 11f.
19. Malachi 4:1f. (3:19f.); Exodus 16:10; Leviticus 9:23; 16:2; Numbers 14:10, 16:19, 42; 20:6; Deuteronomy 31:15.

forth to act in the exercise of his sovereignty.[20] Also, the dual colum-
nar formation assumed by the Glory-cloud as pillar of cloud and pillar
of fire is conceptualized in the Bible as the feet of God standing as
divine witness.[21]

Special interest attaches to the appearance of the Glory-Spirit in a
witness role in historical episodes or visionary scenes of re-creation
that are repetitive of the original creation as described in Genesis 1:2.
For besides confirming our identification of the Glory-Presence in
Genesis 1:2, such evidence of the presence of God as a divine witness
in Genesis 1:2 is an index of the covenantal cast of the whole creation
narrative. Here we can simply suggest some of the data. In the exodus
re-creation, the Glory-cloud, described by Moses by means of the
imagery of Genesis 1:2, as we have seen, stood as pillar witness to the
covenant that defined the legal nature of this redemptive action of
God.[22] At the beginning of the new creation, at the baptism of Jesus,
the Spirit descending over the waters in avian form, as in Genesis 1:2,
was a divine testimony to the Son,[23] the Son who was given as God's
covenant to the people. At the consummation of the new covenant with
its new exodus-creation, the Glory-figure, apocalyptically revealed in
Revelation 10:1ff., is seen clothed with a cloud, rainbow haloed, with
face like the sun and feet like pillars of fire, standing astride creation
with his hand raised in oath to heaven, swearing by him who on the
seventh day finished his creating of the heaven, the earth, the sea, and
all their hosts that in the days of the seventh trumpet the mystery of
God will be finished.[24] In the interpretive light of such redemptive
reproductions of the Genesis 1:2 scene, we see that the Spirit at the
beginning overarched creation as a divine witness to the Covenant of
Creation, as a sign that creation existed under the aegis of his covenant
lordship. Here is the background for the later use of the rainbow as a

---

20. See further, Meredith M. Kline, "The Holy Spirit as Covenant Witness," pp.
19ff., 132ff.
21. Cf. SBA, pp. 200f. The ark of the covenant located beneath the enthroned Glory is
accordingly called God's footstool (Isa. 60:13).
22. Haggai 2:5. Cf. SBA, pp. 201f.
23. Matthew 3:16f.; Luke 3:22; cf. Luke 1:35; 9:31ff.
24. Cf. Revelation 4:2-11.

sign of God's covenant with the earth (Gen. 9:12ff.). And this appointment of the rainbow as covenant sign in turn corroborates the
interpretation of the corresponding supernatural light-and-clouds phenomenon of the Glory (the rainbow character of which is explicit in
some instances[25]) as a sign of the Covenant of Creation.

There are still other ways in which the Glory is conceptualized in the
Scriptures, such as the name-banner and the gate of heaven. But the
aspects of this vastly complex theophanic reality that have been mentioned may suffice for our immediate purposes as we now inquire into
the significance of the archetypal function of the Glory-Spirit in creation, particularly, for the subject of the image of God.

The Glory-Spirit as Archetype

The Glory-Spirit was present at the beginning of creation as a sign of
the *telos* of creation, as the Alpha-archetype of the Omega-Sabbath
that was the goal of creation history.

As an initial step, the Glory functioning as a dynamic paradigm-
power reproduced its own likeness at the mundane level, in the earth-
cosmos. If one is first introduced to the Glory-cloud as it appears in the
later history of God's covenantal reign over Israel, he will probably
identify it as a special, supernatural, localized version of the general
heavenly phenomena of sky and clouds and luminaries. But that will be
seen to be a reversal of the real situation if we recognize the presence
of the Glory-cloud in Genesis 1:2, creatively poised over an earth-
cosmos at a time when light of day and heavenly waters and firmament
had not yet received their name-existence. If we are introduced to the
Glory-cloud at Genesis 1:2 and behold the reproduction of its several
features of light and firmament and clouds transpiring in the creative
process, we will identify the general heavenly phenomena as a rendering in the medium of natural revelation of the supernatural Glory-
heaven. The heavens declare the glory of God in the special sense that
they are a copy of the archetypal Glory of God.

As a result of the creation of the earth-cosmos after the pattern of the
Glory-temple, it has the character of a royal temple of God. Comparing

---

25. See note 17 above.

Israel's temple to his cosmic house, the Lord says: "Heaven is my throne and the earth is my footstool: where is the house that ye build unto me?" (Isa. 66:1).[26] Similarly, the natural heavens consisting of heaven (the firmament) and the heaven of heavens (the cloud waters "above the heaven") are regarded as God's royal chambers and chariot.[27] In harmony with the identification of heaven and earth as a macrocosmic temple, the earthly tabernacle and temple that appear in redemptive re-creation symbolism are designed, as various architectural features show, to be a microcosmic representation of heaven and earth.[28]

A temple design beyond that realized at the mundane level of earth and sea and sky had been conceived by the Creator-Architect. The Glory was a Spirit-temple and the Creator foreknew a temple constructed in spirit-dimensions. As the Omega-point of the creative cloning of the archetypal Glory-temple, the divine design contemplated a living temple of created spirits. God created man in the likeness of the Glory to be a spirit-temple of God in the Spirit. Such is the setting in which the Scriptures introduce man's identity as the earthling made in the image of God.

Once we have recognized the Spirit of the creation narrative as the Glory-Presence, we realize that it is not the case after all that the image-of-God idea appears in Genesis out of the blue, an unexplained riddle inviting nebulously abstract solutions. The statement in Genesis 1:27 that God created man in his own image instead finds a concretely specific and in fact a visible point of reference in the Glory-Spirit theophany of Genesis 1:2. This conclusion is enforced by the data in Genesis 1:26 and 2:7, which bring the Spirit of Genesis 1:2 into connection with the act of man's creation.

According to the Genesis 2:7 account, man was made a living soul by a divine inbreathing. That this is to be understood in terms of the vitalizing breath of the Spirit is evident from the quickening function attributed to the Spirit in Scripture, sometimes in passages reflective of Genesis 2:7. According to Psalm 104:29-31, when God sends forth his Spirit-Glory-Face, the face of the earth is renewed and living creatures

---

26. Cf. II Chronicles 6:18; Matthew 5:34f.
27. Cf. Psalms 11:4; 68:4(5); 93; 103:19; 104:1-3; 115:16; 148:1-4; Isaiah 40:21-23.
28. See further the next chapter.

are created. In Lamentations 4:20, "the breath ($r\hat{u}^a h$) of our nostrils" stands in appositional parallelism to "the (Spirit-) anointed of the Lord." In the vision of Ezekiel 37, when God summons his Spirit-wind to breathe upon the lifeless in the valley, the valley comes to life with a host of living men (vv. 1–10, 14).[29] At the coming into the world of the second Adam, it was revealed to his mother: "The Holy Spirit will come upon you and the Power of the Highest will over-shadow you; therefore also that holy thing which shall be born of you shall be called the Son of God" (Luke 1:35). And when our Lord prophetically portrayed his creation of the new man(kind), he breathed on the disciples and said, "Receive the Holy Spirit" (John 20:22). Clearly then we are to understand that it was the Spirit-Glory of Genesis 1:2 who had hovered over the lifeless deep-and-darkness, sovereignly blowing where he would to bring the world into life, who was the divine breath that fathered the living man-son in Genesis 2:7.

In Genesis 1:26 it is the plural form of the creative fiat that links the creation of man in the image of God to the Spirit-Glory of Genesis 1:2. The Glory-cloud curtains the heavenly enthronement of God in the midst of the judicial council of his celestial hosts. Here is the explanation of the "let us" and the "our image" in the Creator's decree to make man. He was addressing himself to the angelic council of elders, taking them into his deliberative counsel.

This understanding of the first-person-plural fiat is supported by the fact that consistently where this usage occurs in divine speech it is in the context of the heavenly council or at least of heavenly beings. Especially pertinent for Genesis 1:26 is the nearby instance in Genesis 3:22, a declaration concerned again with man's image-likeness to God: "Man has become like one of us to know good and evil." The cherubim mentioned in verse 24 were evidently being addressed. In the cases where God determines to descend and enter into judgment with a city like Babel or Sodom, and a plural form (like "Let us go down") alternates with a singular,[30] the explanation of the plural is at hand in the angelic figures who accompany the Angel of the Lord on his

---

29. Cf. John 3:8.
30. Genesis 11:7 and 18:21.

judicial mission.[31] When, in Isaiah's call experience, the Lord, enthroned in the Glory-cloud of his temple, asks, "Whom shall I send and who will go for us?" (Isa. 6:8), the plural is again readily accounted for by the seraphim attendants at the throne or (if the seraphim are to be distinguished from the heavenly elders, as are the winged creatures of the throne in Revelation 4) by the divine council, which in any case belongs to the scene.[32]

The use of the idiom of the divine council in the Genesis 1:26 fiat thus alerts us to the involvement of the Glory-Spirit in this episode. Those who have sought to explain the plural as a reflection of the trinitarian nature of God and in particular as an allusion to the Spirit of Genesis 1:2, though missing the proper explanation found in the council idiom, have been correct in finding the antecedent of the Genesis 1:26 usage in the Spirit of Genesis 1:2. The Glory theophany, in which God was present as Logos-Wisdom and Spirit-Power, stood as archetype at the creation of man as God's image.

As Genesis 2:7 pictures it, the Spirit-Archetype actively fathered his human ectype. Image of God and son of God are thus twin concepts. This reading of that event in terms of a father-son model and the conceptual bond of the image and son ideas are put beyond doubt by the record of the birth of Seth in Genesis 5:1-3. There, a restatement of Adam's creation in the likeness of God is juxtaposed to a statement that Adam begat a son in his own likeness. Unmistakably, the father-son relationship of Adam and Seth is presented as a proper analogue for understanding the Creator-man relationship[33] and clearly man's likeness to the Creator-Spirit is thus identified as the likeness of a son derived from his father.[34]

---

31. Genesis 18:2 and 19:1.
32. A similar use of the first person plural is characteristic of address in the assembly of the gods as described in Canaanite texts of the Mosaic age.
33. Cf. Luke 3:38.
34. For the connection between the divine image and fatherhood-sonship see Romans 8:29; Hebrews 1:2f.; James 3:9; I John 3:2; cf. Luke 20:36. By setting the image-likeness formula in the context of sonship, Genesis 5:1-3 contradicts the suggestion that the image idea is a matter of representative status rather than of representational likeness or resemblance. For Seth was not Adam's representative, but as Adam's son he did resemble his father. The terminology "in his likeness" serves as the equivalent in human procreation of the phrase "after its kind" which is used for plant and animal reproduction and of course refers to resemblance.

Relating what has been said of the presence of the Son of God in the Glory theophany of Genesis 1 to the role of the Glory-Spirit in the creation of man as son-image, it appears that there was a specific divine archetypal referent for the sonship aspect of God's image in man. The eternal, firstborn Son furnished a pattern for man as a royal glory-image of the Father.[35] It was in his creative action as the Son, present in the Glory-Spirit, making man in his own son-image that the Logos revealed himself as the One in whom was the life that is the light of men.[36] Not first as incarnate Word breathing on men the Spirit and re-creating them in his heavenly image, but at the very beginning he was quickening Spirit, creating man after his image and glory.

Indeed, the Son does do his creative work anew and consummatingly in redemptive history, and an introductory exploration of this will be relevant here. For to observe how Scripture portrays the re-creation as a process wherein the Glory-Son fashions the new man(kind) in his own Glory-likeness is surely to find biblical confirmation of the interpretation of the original creation as a making of man in the likeness of the Glory-Spirit.

This theme of the re-creation of the new man(kind) by the Lord of glory in his own likeness is prominent and, in fact, foundational in the Book of Revelation.[37] This book as a whole depicts the messianic redemptive re-creation in symbolism drawn from the Mosaic reenactment of creation in the exodus, but that layer of the Apocalyptic representation overlies a foundational conceptual structure derived from the original creation event. Inevitably so, since creation provides the basic mold filled by redemption.

The opening vision of the Book of Revelation reveals Christ as the archetypal Glory-image and the book closes with a prophetic view of the church as the ectypal image. In the Spirit, John saw Christ in the form of a theophanic blend of the Glory-Spirit and the Angel of the Presence with the anthropomorphic lineaments of the latter dominant

---

35. It is not necessary to take *charaktēr* in Hebrews 1:3 in the sense of a seal-pattern used to impress something else with its own image in order to conclude that the Creator fashioned his human son in the likeness of the divine Son. In the analogue to man's image-sonship found in the sonship of the divine Son, the correspondence consists simply in the idea of likeness, the resemblance of a son to a father, apart from any idea of derivation or subordination.

36. Cf. John 1:4.

37. A more textured picture of this will be found in the following chapters.

and the Glory-cloud features adjectival. The theophanic figure was, further, a blend of the "ancient of days" as well as the "son of man" of Daniel 7:9ff., and thus fully trinitarian. Earlier, at the transfiguration, John had been witness to a proleptic apocalypse of Christ in his majestic glory. The resurrection marked Christ's definitive assumption of his Spirit identity[38] and, in the vision of Revelation 1, John saw this risen, glorified Christ as the Spirit-Lord, present to re-create all things and particularly to impart his glory to his church, the new man re-created in his image.

This new work of creation is also a covenantal process, as are all God's works. Accordingly, Christ the Creator, "the Alpha and Omega, the beginning and the ending, the first and the last" (Rev. 1:8) is introduced by John as "the faithful witness" (Rev. 1:5) and identifies himself as "the Amen, the faithful and true witness, the beginning of the creation of God" (Rev. 3:14).[39] He appears in this vision of re-creation as the One who came to his church in the Spirit at Pentecost, standing as the Spirit-witness to the new covenant as earlier he stood witness to the old covenant in the Glory-cloud at Sinai, and still earlier to the creation covenant in the Glory-Spirit of Genesis 1:2.

John beheld the transfigured Lord as the light of the world, his countenance like the sun, in the midst of the derivative, reflective light of the seven golden lamps representative of the seven churches. These symbolic circumstances attested to the Lord's covenantal purpose to fashion his church in the radiant image of his own glory. This prospect he articulated in his promises to the overcomers in his letters to the churches, for these promises describe just so many facets of the glory of the living Lord.

The covenanted hope of the creational process is seen in its sabbatical realization at the close of the Apocalypse. All the elements of the separate glory promises to the overcomers are gathered together and the symbolism fully elaborated in the closing vision(s) of the glorified church. It is not the new mankind alone that is in view; the vision is a panorama of cosmic re-creation. The depiction of this corresponds closely to the account of creation in Genesis 1. A new heaven and earth

---

38. Cf. Richard B. Gaffin, Jr., *The Centrality of the Resurrection: A Study in Paul's Soteriology* (Grand Rapids: Baker, 1978), p. 126.
39. Cf. Revelation 19:11, 13; 21:5; 22:6.

are seen, replacing the first (Rev. 21:1a; cf. Gen. 1:1). Then the deep-and-darkness condition, the not-yet-hospitable stage of Genesis 1:2a, has its negative reflection in the statement of Revelation 21:1a that there is no more sea in the new cosmos. And answering to the Spirit-cloud, the archetypal temple over the earth in Genesis 1:2b, is the temple-city of Revelation 21:2, seen descending out of the heavens.

New Jerusalem as portrayed in Revelation 21 and 22 is the ultimate likeness of the Spirit-Glory, for it is a city transfigured in light and its light is the glory of God (21:11; 23; 22:5); it is the tabernacle of God (21:3), the cuboid holy of holies where the "Alpha and Omega, the beginning and the end," who sits above the cherubim of the Glory-cloud, is seen enthroned (21:5, 6). In this New Jerusalem all the promises of the letters to the seven churches find their Amen in Christ. Here all is fulfilled. Christ, the archetypal Glory-image of the opening vision, has created the new mankind in his glory-likeness. Christ, the archetypal temple, has constructed the church into a temple for God's presence. And in this new reality of the union of the new man, the church, with the new man, Christ, more is involved in the church's likeness to the divine Glory than mere reflection of that Glory. There is a mysterious kind of identification with the Glory in the Spirit. The city-temple that shines with the glory of God is the Glory theophany with the church-body of Christ engrafted into it. For while the church is the temple where God dwells, God is the Spirit-Temple where the church dwells (Rev. 21:22).

Thus the Apocalypse of Jesus Christ interprets to us the apocalypse of Elohim in Genesis 1 and clarifies our view of the Spirit in Genesis 1 as the theophanic Glory, the divine archetype for the creation of man in the image of God.[40]

Toward a Reconstruction of the Image-of-God Concept

If, according to the Genesis creation narrative, the Glory theophany was the paradigm of the image of God borne by man, one would expect

---

40. That the Apocalyptic symbolism is a treatment of precisely the image-of-God idea, as portrayed in the Old and New Testaments under the figures of priestly investiture and prophetic transfiguration, will be more fully demonstrated in the following chapters.

glory to be a prominent aspect of the image idea throughout the Bible. In checking this out, it will be useful to have before us a brief ana- lytical review of the composition of the complex Glory theophany. Nuclear to the divine Glory is its official-functional aspect: it is the glory of royal-judicial office. In the Glory, God sits as King. This official royal glory comes to formal-physical expression in theophanic radiance; in the Glory, God is enthroned in majestic robes of light. There is also an ethical dimension to the Glory: the foundations of the cloud-veiled throne are justice and righteousness, and fidelity and truth go before it in royal procession.[41] It is a throne of holiness[42] and the enthroned King of glory is ever acclaimed as "holy, holy, holy" by the multitude of the heavenly host (Isa. 6:3).

Only a cursory survey of the more salient data will be necessary to show that these central aspects of the Glory theophany are indeed dominant in the biblical contexts in which the image-of-God theme emerges.

In the creative fiat addressed to the heavenly council, "Let us make man in our image," angels are identified as sharing in the image- likeness to God.[43] The lines of likeness connect not only God and man but God and angels, and man and angels. Agreeably, in the reflection of Genesis 1:26ff. in Psalm 8:5ff., man's likeness to God is expounded in a comparison of man and angels.[44] That man in his likeness to God is like members of the divine council suggests that to bear the image of God is to participate in the judicial function of the divine Glory. And it is this judicial role that is prominent when the image idea next appears in Genesis 3:22. There, man's likeness to God is expressed in terms of his knowing good and evil, which has to do with the royal function of judicial discernment and decision rendering. The latter is elsewhere noted as a mark of likeness to both God and angels.[45]

Attention is drawn to the royal-office element in the image of God by the conjunction of references to the image and to man's dominion over the world in both the fiat and fulfillment sections of the record of

---

41. Psalms 89:14; 97:2.
42. Psalm 47:8.
43. Hence, too, a designation of angels found in council contexts is "sons of God" (Job 1:6; 2:1; 38:7; Pss. 29:1; 89:6).
44. Cf. Hebrews 2:7.
45. I Kings 3:28, cf. 9; II Samuel 14:17.

man's creation in Genesis 1:26–28. Moreover, when commenting on this record and identifying man as one made a little lower than the angels, Psalm 8 reflects on the majestic splendor with which the Creator crowned man and the universal reign assigned to him.

Where the image-of-God idea again emerges in Genesis beyond the first three chapters, the kingly aspect continues to be prominent. In Genesis 5:1f., man's creation as divine image-bearer is recalled by way of introducing a major section of the book (Gen. 5:1–6:8) that reaches its climax in the account of "the sons of God," or "sons of the gods," the tyrant kings whose evil reign precipitated the flood (Gen. 6:1ff.).[46] The reference to the image-of-God idea in the formulaic heading of Genesis 5:1f. is then especially meaningful, in effect establishing in the general royal office that belongs to man by virtue of his creation in God's image the foundation for the special office of king that arises in the subsequent history.[47] The same point is made in the other passage in the Book of Genesis where the divine image is mentioned. In Genesis 9:6, the fact that God created man in his image is cited as the reason that man is assigned the solemn judicial responsibility of discerning between good and evil in a case of murder and particularly of executing the guilty. As image of God, man is a royal son with the judicial function appertaining to kingly office.

Glory is again to the fore when the Scriptures speak of man's re-creation in God's image. The renewal of the divine image in men is an impartation to them of the likeness of the archetypal glory of Christ. We have observed this in the Book of Revelation. In II Corinthians 4:6, Christ, the glory-image of God (cf. II Cor. 4:4) is likened to the archetypal Glory-Spirit-Face of Genesis 1:2 as the apostle Paul draws the parallel between the light of God's glory in the face of Christ, the light that now shines in our hearts, and the light that shone in the darkness over which the Spirit hovered at the creation (Gen. 1:3).

The mode of the impartation of Christ's glory in image renewal is described according to various figurative models appropriate to Christ's identity either as Spirit-Lord[48] or as second Adam. Man's

---

46. See my "Divine Kingship and Genesis 6:1-4," *The Westminster Theological Journal* 24 (1962): 187-204.

47. See my "Oracular Origin of the State" in *Biblical and Near Eastern Studies,* ed. Gary A. Tuttle (Grand Rapids: Eerdmans, 1978): pp. 132-41.

48. Cf. Romans 1:3f.; I Corinthians 15:45; II Corinthians 3:17.

reception of the divine image from Christ, the Glory-Presence, is depicted as a transforming vision of the Glory and as an investiture with the Glory. Moses is the Old Testament model for the former and Aaron for the latter.[49] Beholding the Sinai revelation of the Glory-Face transformed the face of Moses so that he reflectively radiated the divine Glory. So we, beholding the glory of the Spirit-Lord, are transformed into the same image (II Cor. 3:7-18; 4:4-6). When the investiture figure is used, what is "put on" is the new man created in the image of God (Eph. 4:24; Col. 3:10), or Christ the Lord (Rom. 13:14; Gal. 3:27; cf. Eph. 2:15; 4:13), or the resurrection glory of immortality (I Cor. 15:53.; II Cor. 5:2ff.). An equivalency of the image and glory ideas is again indicated by this series of passages. To be noted also is the ethical characterization of the image in Ephesians 4:24 and Colossians 3:10 in terms of holiness, righteousness, and truth or knowledge, the characteristic qualities of the Glory throne of judgment.

In the vocabulary of Peter, "partakers of the divine nature" expresses renewal in the image of God (II Peter 1:4).[50] In the context of this expression in II Peter 1, the figures of reflective transformation and of investiture are both found, the former with reference to the transfiguration of Jesus into the radiant likeness of the overshadowing Glory (vv. 16ff.) and the latter in reference to Peter's anticipated death, described as a divestiture, a negative counterpart to the resurrection investiture with glory (v. 14). But whatever mode of achieving participation in "the divine nature" is contemplated in verse 4, here too the divine image is identified with the divine glory. For this participation in the divine nature spoken of in verse 4 answers to the divine calling to God's own glory and splendor[51] mentioned in verse 3.

When Christ's identity as second Adam is in view, figures appropriate to the position and role of the first Adam are used to explain transmission of the image of Christ (and thus of God). In I Corinthians 15 we are told that just as descent from the first Adam means for all mankind—as it did for Seth (Gen. 5:3)—to bear Adam's earthly im-

---

49. The next two chapters will develop at length these two symbolic models of the *imago Dei*, the prophetic and the priestly.
50. Cf. James 3:9.
51. In I Peter 2:9, *aretē* is used of Israel, chosen to declare the splendor of him who calls out of darkness into his wonder-light. In the Septuagint, it is used for the divine Glory (*hôd*) in Habakkuk 3:3.

age, so "descent" from the second man means to bear his heavenly image (I Cor. 15:47–49). Shifting the angle of the family analogy, Christ is said to be the first-born of many brethren who are predestined to be conformed to his image, and therefore to be glorified (Rom. 8:29, 30; Heb. 2:8–12). In Philippians 3:21, Christ's bestowing of the likeness of his glory-image on his people is interpreted in terms of the historical mandate given to the first Adam to exercise dominion over all things and subdue the earth. For Christ's refashioning of our bodies into his heavenly glory-likeness is described as an exercise of his power whereby he is able to subdue all things to himself.[52]

In sum, what we find is that the biblical exposition of the image of God is consistently in terms of a glory like the Glory of God. The apostle Paul brings it all into focus when he describes men as "the image and glory of God" (I Cor. 11:7).

From the foregoing it appears that much of the traditional discussion of the image-of-God concept has been out of contact with a biblical base. What has traditionally been regarded as a broad, permanent layer of the image is not in immediate view at all when the Scriptures speak of the image of God. And the ethical *conformitas*, regarded as the narrower aspect of the image in the classical view, requires reorientation to take its place as one element in a doctrine of the image that seeks to build with components taken over unchanged, directly from their biblical source. Also, the traditional avoidance of the visible corporeal aspect of man in formulating the *imago Dei* doctrine (in deference to the noncorporeal, invisible nature of God) has not reckoned adequately with the fact of theophanic revelation and in particular has missed the theophanic referent of the image in the Genesis 1 context.

Image and glory appear as twin models in the Bible for expressing man's likeness to the divine Original. If they are to be distinguished, the distinction might be that image-likeness is reproduction of the original and glory-likeness is reflection of the original. Or, that image is stative and expresses the fact of imageness, i.e., that man is secondary, not the original but different from it because of his createdness, while glory is active and expresses the content of the image, i.e., that

---

52. Cf. I Corinthians 15:24f.

man is similar to God in those features comprised by the concept of glory. To the extent that such distinctions are valid, the aspect of discontinuity connoted by image and the aspect of continuity suggested by glory are mutually conditioning, correlative aspects of man's likeness to God. Both image and glory mean likeness. Moreover, such is their equivalency that where all that constitutes the glory is gone, no vestige of the image remains.

Though image-likeness is terminable, it is otherwise constant. The glory aspect of man's God-likeness, on the other hand, is variable; it is subject to degrees of reduction as well as to termination and it also may undergo intensification and expansion in the historical-eschatological process.

Under the concept of man as the glory-image of God the Bible includes functional (or official), formal (or physical), and ethical components, corresponding to the composition of the archetypal Glory. Functional glory-likeness is man's likeness to God in the possession of official authority and in the exercise of dominion. Ethical glory is reflection of the holiness, righteousness, and truth of the divine Judge (not just the presence of a moral faculty of any religious orientation whatsoever). And formal-physical glory-likeness is man's bodily reflection of the theophanic and incarnate Glory.

Man as created was already crowned with glory and honor, for made in the likeness of the enthroned Glory, a little lower than the angels of the divine council, man was invested with official authority to exercise dominion as priest-king in God's earthly courts. Yet, the glory of man's royal functioning would be progressive as he increasingly fulfilled his historical task of subduing the earth, his ultimate attainment of functional glory awaiting the eschatological glorification of his whole nature after the image of the radiant Glory-Spirit. Ethical glory also belonged to man as created and in this respect man would have gone from glory to glory had he not sinned, moving on from a state of simple righteousness to one of confirmed righteousness.

Man in the Fall became destitute of the glory of God (Rom. 3:23)—at least such was the effect of the Fall apart from the intervention of divine grace. Actually, by the common grace of God, a measure of the glory-image was preserved in spite of the Fall. Scriptural references to postlapsarian man as still the image of God (Gen. 9:6; James 3:9) show that man continues to be the image of God after the Fall and that he is so even without personal experience of redemptive renewal. According to Genesis 3:22, man had in the very course of the Fall manifested the official-functional glory he had been given by engaging in judicial action after the manner of the divine council. Of course, he did so in such a way as to be guilty of gross malfeasance and forfeited his right to continue in office. But by the common grace of God this official glory of man was perpetuated and constitutes the primary if not the total basis for the Bible's attribution of image-of-God status to fallen man even apart from re-creation in Christ. By falling into sin, man lost his ethical glory. The covering of glory was replaced by the nakedness of shame. Though still possessed of an official glory by common grace, man was stripped of righteousness, holiness, and love of the truth. Whatever semblance of ethical glory was maintained by common grace, such does not clearly figure in the Bible's identification of postlapsarian man as still the image of God. Fallen man is a naked image.

Man re-created in the image of God is restored to the hope of the formal-physical image-glory of resurrection immortality and Spiritual existence. Meanwhile, God, who has prepared for the new man the covering of eternal glory, gives him the earnest of the Spirit (II Cor. 5:5). In his redemptive renewal man is re-created after the image of God in true knowledge, righteousness, and holiness (Eph. 4:24; Col. 3:10) and with respect to this ethical glory-likeness to God man is transformed from glory to glory by the Spirit of the Lord (II Cor. 3:18; 4:16; Rom. 12:2). Beyond the official-functional glory the new man has in the realm of common grace, he has through his union with Christ in the Spirit a part in Christ's enthronement in the heavenly sphere (Eph. 2:6). In this respect too there is movement from glory to glory, for the blessedness of Christian death is the "first resurrection," the intermediate state, where the believer, perfect in righteousness, is present with Christ to live and reign with him (Rev. 20:4-6),[53] and beyond the second (i.e., bodily) resurrection the overcomers, possessed of the

---

53. See my "The First Resurrection," *The Westminster Theological Journal* 37 (1975): 366-75; and "The First Resurrection: A Reaffirmation," *The Westminster Theological Journal* 39 (1976): 110-19.

fulness of formal and ethical glory, participate with the enthroned Christ in the consummation of man's official royal glory (Rev. 3:21).

Such is the historical-eschatological variableness of the image-glory of God in man. Concerning the reprobate, biblical warrant is lacking to ascribe to them in the condition of second death even the status of naked image. This is not to deny that they continue to be human beings, for image of God and humanness, it must be remembered, are not simple equivalents.

No more successful than the classical approach to the *imago Dei* is the view of Karl Barth. His position not only fails to account for the pervasive equation of the image and glory concepts throughout the Scriptures, but the primary exegetical argument for it, an appeal to Genesis 1:27 and 5:1f., is specious. From the fact that the declaration of man's creation in God's likeness is followed in these verses by the statement that man was created male and female (1:27c and 5:2a) the notion is drawn that it is human existence as male-female that constitutes man's image-likeness to God, a human analogue to the fellowship within the plurality of God's being. But even if Genesis 1:27c and 5:2a were taken with the preceding image statements in 1:27a and b and in 5:1b and c respectively, it could not be simply assumed that the intention was to define the content of the image idea. The purpose might rather be to identify men and women alike as being individually the image of God.

Actually, Genesis 1:27c and 5:2a are to be taken not (directly) with what precedes them, but with what follows. This is evident from considerations of structure, style, and sense. Structurally, the absence of the male-female statement from the fiat section of the fiat-fulfillment pattern in Genesis 1:26–28 speaks against taking it as the essential exposition of the image idea, especially since the dominion idea does find a place along with that of the image in the fiat as well as fulfillment section. Stylistically, Genesis 1:27a and b forms a complete synonymous parallelism apart from 1:27c, which is linked to what follows by the use of the third plural pronoun. In Genesis 5, the structural tie of verse 2a with the following word of blessing is, if anything, even more evident than in Genesis 1:27. And as for the sense, the observation that man was created male and female is obviously an apt introduction to the following procreation blessing in 1:28

and 5:2b. The latter would in fact be much too abrupt without the preparatory sexual identification of man. On the other hand, if the intent had been as the exegesis controverted here supposes, the choice of the biological terminology, "male and female," would not have been happy; "man and woman" would have been more appropriate. It is only as (an introductory) part of the following statement of man's cultural task of filling and subduing the earth (Gen. 1:28; 5:2b) that Genesis 1:27c and 5:2a refer back to 1:27a and b and 5:1 respectively, so that not man's male-female composition but his royal dominion is what explicates the image idea in these verses.

In I Corinthians 11:7ff., Paul does expound the man-woman relationship as an instance of the image-glory pattern. However, he interprets the man(husband)-woman(wife) relationship not as that which itself constitutes man(kind)'s image-likeness to God, but, on the contrary (and excluding that possibility), as simply containing an analogy to the image of God in man. It is not that the man-woman relationship is an image-likeness of intertrinitarian relationships, but that the man-woman relationship mirrors the glory-reflecting relationship of mankind to God in which the image of God in mankind actually does consist.[54]

The analogy to the image-of-God idea that is involved in the man-woman relationship is, according to the apostle's teaching, that the woman, as one derived from the man in creational origin, is the glory of the man, just as mankind, both man and woman, as creational offspring of the Spirit-Glory, is God's reflective glory-image. Womanhood is thus viewed in Scripture as another analogue, along with human sonship (cf. Gen. 5:1, 2), of mankind's image status as derivative and consequently subject to authority. It is evident how far from the biblical data they have wandered who would find in a supposed appointment of an egalitarian marital relationship a reflection of interdivine relationships and would then identify that as the image of God. What we do find here in the Bible's use of the womanhood analogy for the image-of-God nature of mankind is further confirmation of the equivalency of the ideas of image and glory.

---

54. Wherever the man(husband)-woman(wife) relationship is used in the Bible as a figure of a divine relationship, that relationship is always one between God and man; it is never used as an analogue of interdivine fellowship.

Chapter Two

A Priestly Model of the Image of God

Re-creation in the image of God is, according to one biblical metaphor, an act of investiture. Those who are renewed in the divine likeness are said to "put on" the new man or Christ or resurrection glory.[1] Mixing the metaphor, Paul speaks of the perfecting of the divine image at the resurrection as a being clothed with a heavenly tabernacle-house (II Cor. 5:1-4). This curious combination of sartorial and architectural imagery provides a clue to the source of the investiture figure in the symbolism of the Old Testament cult.

The Tabernacle—A Replica of the Glory-Spirit

The earth-cosmos was made after the archetypal pattern of the Glory-Spirit referred to in Genesis 1:2 and accordingly is viewed in Scripture as a cosmic royal residence or temple.[2] Heaven and earth were established as a holy palace of the Creator-King, with the heaven of heavens in particular corresponding to the Glory-cloud as the seat of his sovereignty.

Then, preparing a place for the man-priest who was to be created, the Lord God produced in Eden a microcosmic version of his cosmic sanctuary. The garden planted there was holy ground with guardianship of its sanctity committed in turn to men and to cherubim.[3] It was the temple-garden of God,[4] the place chosen by the Glory-Spirit

---

1. Romans 13:14; I Corinthians 15:53f.; II Corinthians 5:2ff.; Galatians 3:27; Ephesians 4:24; Colossians 3:10. See p. 29.
2. See. p. 20.
3. Genesis 2:15; 3:24.
4. Isaiah 51:3; Ezekiel 28:13, 16; 31:9.

who hovered over creation from the beginning to be the focal site of his throne-presence among men.

Such was evidently Ezekiel's reading of Genesis 2. In the passage where he compares the Prince of Tyre to a figure in the original paradise scene (Ezek. 28:14, 16), he speaks of a covering[5] cherub as present there on the holy mountain of God. The Glory theophany thus located by Ezekiel in Eden is prominent in his apocalyptic vision of paradise restored and consummated.[6] The same is true of the Johannine treatment of this theme.[7] Particularly interesting for its backward illumination of the Edenic prototype is Isaiah's picture of the eschatological kingdom as a paradise created anew under the heavenly tent-covering of divine Glory:[8] "Over the entire holy site of Mount Zion and its assemblies Yahweh will create a cloud by day and the bright smoke of a flaming fire by night—truly a covering[9] canopy of glory over all of it. And it will be continually a shade from the heat and a sheltering refuge and hiding place from the storm and rain" (Isa. 4:5, 6).

By virtue of the presence of this theophanic cloud-canopy, Eden had the character of a holy tabernacle, a microcosmic house of God. And since it was God himself who, present in his theophanic Glory, constituted the Edenic temple, man in the Garden of God could quite literally confess that Yahweh was his refuge and the Most High was his habita-

---

5. The same word (*sākak*) is used for the guardian-covering function of this cherub as is used in Psalm 91:4 for the Glory theophany with which winged cherubim are associated: "He shall cover thee with his feathers, and under his wings shalt thou trust." In Exodus 25:20 *sākak* is used for the covering of the ark by the outstretched wings of the golden cherubim. The fiery stones (or "sons of fire") mentioned along with the cherub in Ezekiel 28 also belong to the Glory-cloud imagery (Isa. 6:6; Ezek. 1:13; 10:2; Ps. 18:8–14 [9–15]).

6. Ezekiel 43:2ff.

7. Revelation 21 and 22.

8. Isaiah 4:2–6; cf. 28:5f. The use of *bārā'* (Isa. 4:5), the distinctive verb of creation in Genesis 1:1, makes clear the allusion to the original creation and, of interest for our interpretation of Genesis 1:2 (see pp. 14ff.), the object of *bārā'* is the Glory-cloud, Moreover, the identification of the Glory theophany with the Spirit is found here, as in Genesis 1:2. For Isaiah 4:4 identifies the Spirit as the fiery instrument of the judgment prerequisite to Zion's glorification and this is the same divine agency mentioned in verse 5 as Zion's fiery cloud covering.

9. The Glory-cloud is called a *sukkāh*, "covering, pavilion"; cf. note 5 above.

tion.[10] Reviewing man and his world back to creation's beginnings, Moses in Psalm 90 acknowledges that the Lord, present as the theophanic temple above the unbounded deep before ever the earth was formed or the mountains brought forth (v. 2), has been man's "dwelling place in all generations" (v. 1). And, using the popular poetic device of inclusion, Moses returns at the close of the Psalm to his opening theme, praying that the Shekinah Glory,[11] the tabernacle of Eden, might continue to appear in its beauty[12] over God's covenant people (vv. 16, 17).

The history of the exodus, culminating in the building of the tabernacle, is so recounted as to bring out its nature as a redemptive re-enactment of creation. In this re-creation event the Glory theophany is again viewed as a sanctuary-canopy[13] and it is found to function again as a creative paradigm.[14] It hovers at the top of Sinai over the wilderness-*tōhû*[15] and reproduces its likeness in the world below. At the foot of Sinai the tabernacle appears, made according to the archetypal pattern seen on the mount, designed to be a replica of the Glory-Spirit-temple.

One way the record of this event in the Book of Exodus recalls the account of the original creation in Genesis is its adoption of the fiat-fulfillment structure of the day-stanzas of Genesis 1 as the format for its account of the building of the tabernacle. Exodus 25–31 presents the divine fiat-commands and Exodus 35–40 contains the corresponding account of fulfillment. This pattern repeats within the narrative of the actual setting up of the tabernacle in Exodus 40: the divine directives are given first in verses 1–15, and then the execution, item by item, is described in verses 16–33. In the account of the preparation of the various components of the tabernacle and again in the account of

---

10. Psalm 91:2, 9.
11. On *hādār*, cf. Psalms 29:4; 96:6; 104:1; Isaiah 2:10, 19, 21. In the Ugaritic Keret epic (155), *hdrt* is used for a dream-theophany.
12. On *nōʿam*, cf. Psalm 27:4.
13. Hence, prophetic descriptions of the Glory-tabernacle of the consummation draw upon the theophanic phenomena of Mount Sinai and Mount Zion for their contributions of typological details to that picture. See Isaiah 4 again in this connection.
14. See pp. 20ff.
15. Deuteronomy 32:10.

the assembling of them into the finished tabernacle (Exod. 35–40) the connection between the divine word and the performance of it is underscored by the repeated reminder that the work was carried out according to God's commandment.[16]

The Sabbath motif that informs Genesis 1:1–2:3 is prominent in the account of the tabernacle. The completion of the project is related in a concluding summary (Exod. 40:33; cf. 39:43) that echoes the seventh day conclusion of the creation record in Genesis 2:2. The promulgation of the Sabbath ordinance marks the close of the fiat-command section (31:12–17) and the beginning of the fulfillment section (35:2, 3). And the consecration of the cult is a seven-day process.[17]

The Spirit who structured the cosmic temple in the beginning by divine wisdom[18] was also the primary builder of the tabernacle, present and acting through Bezalel and Oholiab, whom he filled and endued with the wisdom of craftsmanship.[19] In this connection the creative naming theme of Genesis 1 also emerges.[20]

Another parallel between the original and the Sinaitic creation episodes is that both include climactically the fashioning of man in the image of the Glory-Spirit.[21] In the Exodus record this receives two-fold expression. There is the transfiguring of Moses through his "face to face" communion with the Glory-Presence so that his face reflected the glory-likeness of the divine Glory.[22] And there is the investiture of Aaron in the likeness of the Glory-Spirit. Like the Genesis 1:26, 27 record of the creation of man in the image of God, the Exodus account of Aaron's image-investiture follows the pattern of fiat-command (Exod. 28 and 29) and fulfillment (Exod. 39:1ff. and 40:12ff.). Here we are touching on the central theme of the present chapter, but, at this point, simply as one of the significant features in the creation pattern which informs the narrative of the founding of Israel's cult at Sinai.[23]

---

16. See especially Exodus 39 and 40.
17. Exodus 29:37; 34:18.
18. Cf. Proverbs 8:22ff.
19. Exodus 35:30–36:1.
20. Exodus 35:30.
21. See pp. 21ff.
22. Exodus 33:11; 34:29ff.
23. The fact that Aaron's investiture is part of this larger reproduction of the Genesis creation pattern in turn supports the interpretation of the investiture as a symbol of creation in God's image.

A further major aspect of the parallelism between the Genesis and Exodus accounts is that creation in each instance is a covenantal process. In Exodus the building of the tabernacle (Exod. 25–40) is an immediate consequence of the covenant-making that was initiated by the revelation of the Glory-Spirit standing on Sinai as Lord and divine covenant Witness.[24] So too the Genesis creation was constituted a covenantal event by the presence of the same Glory-Spirit standing over the waters (Gen. 1:2) as sanctioning Witness-Lord.

Under the Covenant of Creation a holy cosmic order was produced that had its focus and core in the microcosmic Edenic sanctuary. Similarly, the Sinaitic Covenant instituted a holy kingdom-order with a focus in the Mosaic tabernacle. From the whole historical-literary parallelism that we have observed between the original creation and the exodus re-creation we would naturally expect to find that the Creator-Lord so designed the Mosaic tabernacle that it reflected the nature of the original cosmic and microcosmic temples, and examination of the construction of the tabernacle reveals that such was in fact the case. More particularly, our present concern is to show that the Mosaic tabernacle was a replica of the Glory-Spirit, the archetypal temple itself. Since the Glory theophany is the invisible heavenly temple brought into a veiled pre-consummation form of visibility,[25] what we are affirming about the Mosaic tabernacle is nothing other than what the author of the Book of Hebrews says when he identifies that tabernacle as a copy of heavenly things (Heb. 9:23, 24), an antitype of the greater archetypal tabernacle (Heb. 9:11).

By entering and filling the tabernacle, the Glory theophany identified with it[26] and this Shekinah enthroned above the cherubim in the holy of holies was the clearest possible manifestation of the fact that the tabernacle had been designed to be a symbolic reproduction of the reality of the heavenly temple, where the God of Glory is enthroned in the midst of the angelic divine council.

Various features of the tabernacle further evince this design of symbolically reproducing the Glory-temple. The motif of the heavenly angelic court found in the two golden cherubim above the ark was

---

24. Exodus 19–24. See pp. 19f. and 24f.
25. See p. 17.
26. Exodus 25:22; Psalm 80:1 (2); Isaiah 6:1.

repeated in the cherubim figures portrayed on the inside covering of the tabernacle. And the fiery radiance of the Glory-court was mirrored by the use of flame-colored linen for that inner, cherubim-filled covering.

In imitation of the multiple strata of the cloud formation that enveloped the Glory-fire at Sinai (the darkness, clouds, and heavy clouds),[27] the tabernacle had several layers of coverings. Thus, overlying the inner covering, which corresponded to the inmost cloud-veil about the fire in God's theophanic Glory, was the tent cover of goats' hair,[28] and over that was at least one covering of skins.[29]

Tabernacle-temple architecture also reflected the conceptualization of the Glory formation as the gate of heaven. The cloudy canopy of Glory with its two earthward projecting columns, the pillar of fire and pillar of cloud, formed an entry frame with lintel over two side posts—an entry to heaven. Since the Glory is identified as the Name of Yahweh,[30] the canopy of Glory above the column-posts was also viewed as a standard or name-banner.[31] In the tabernacle's holy of holies, the two cherubim which flanked the ark-footstool with their outspread wings touching above as a firmament-lintel, a banner bearing the Name-Glory of the Spirit enthroned above, formed an entry frame to heaven. This symbolism was duplicated at the entry to the sanctuary. Thus, the two bronze pillars standing at the temple entrance must be related to this pattern, and so too the entrance-way itself.[32]

A reproduction of the Glory-cloud, as we have now seen, the tabernacle also reflected the structure of the cosmos-temple, itself a copy of the Glory-temple. The ark was God's "footstool"[33] and thus corre-

---

27. Deuteronomy 4:11; 5:22; Psalm 97:2.
28. Exodus 26:7ff.
29. Exodus 26:14; 36:19; 40:19. See G. E. Mendenhall, *The Tenth Generation* (Baltimore: The Johns Hopkins University Press, 1973), p. 43, note 35.
30. Deuteronomy 12:5, 11, 21; 14:23, 24; 16:2, 6, 11; 26:2. I Kings 8:29; II Kings 23:27; Psalm 89:12(13). Cf. Phoenician *šm*, "presence".
31. Psalms 20:5(6); 60:4(6); Isaiah 11:12; 49:22; 59:19–60:3. Wooden poles and trees planted by altars were a cultic representation of this; cf. Isaiah 51:16.
32. With the translation of *miptān* corrected to "lintel," an interesting association emerges between the entry lintel and the cherubim throne in Ezekiel's visions (Ezek. 9:3; 10:4, 18), and the picture of the course of the river of life flowing from the throne of God (Ezek. 47:1; cf. Rev. 22:1, 2) is clarified. For the depiction of the winged sun-disk (and equivalent symbols of divine glory) on the lintels of sacred doorways, see Mendenhall, *The Tenth Generation*, p. 49, figure 14 and p. 51, figure 19.
33. I Chronicles 28:2; Psalms 99:5; 132:7; Lamentations 2:1.

sponded to the earth-footstool in the cosmic temple,[34] while the higher region of the holy of holies where the Glory was enthroned in the midst of the cherubim corresponded to the heaven and heaven of heavens.[35] Agreeably, Ezekiel saw the theophanic Glory above a heavenly firmament above the heads of the living creatures.[36] The overall floor plan of the tabernacle with its divisions into outer court, holy place, and holy of holies reproduced on the horizontal plane the sectioning of the cosmic temple into earth, heaven, and heaven of heavens. And each of the tabernacle's three divisions, not just the holy of holies, represented heaven and earth in its vertical dimension, the court standing under the open sky and the holy place, along with the holy of holies, under the symbolic heavens of the tabernacle coverings. The three screens at the court gate, the main temple entrance, and the entrance to the holy of holies are called by the same term for "covering" (māsāk) as is used of the Glory-cloud.[37] Still other architectural features and furnishings of the tabernacle had cosmic significance. The laver in the outer court, for example, was an image of the heavenly sea. Substantiation of the cosmic symbolism of the tabernacle is afforded by the coalescence of the eternal holy of holies, the tabernacle-city, New Jerusalem, with the heaven and earth in John's apocalyptic vision of the new creation (Rev. 21 and 22).

Edenic motifs also appear in the tabernacle, especially in its later temple development and in prophetic pictures of the eschatological tabernacling of God in creation, evidence that the tabernacle was meant to symbolize the redemptive renewal of the paradise-sanctuary as well as the macrocosmic temple of creation. Decorative features of the temple included carvings of flowers, palm trees, and cherubim[38] and in the eschatological sanctuary are found the river and trees of life.[39] In Ezekiel 47 the same verb is used as in Genesis 2 for the

---

34. Isaiah 66:1.
35. Psalm 11:4.
36. Ezekiel 1:22, 25ff. Cf. Exodus 24:10.
37. Psalm 105:39. As described in Exodus 26:33 (cf. Ezek. 42:20), the function of the inner veil was to divide the holy place from the holy of holies, another reminiscence of the Genesis creation narrative, where the dividing function is prominent (Gen. 1:4, 6, 7, 14, 18) and the same verb (bdl) is used. In both Genesis creation and Exodus re-creation accounts the process is one of structuring spheres and positioning objects ("their host," Gen. 2:1) in them.
38. I Kings 6:18; 29, 32, 35; 7:18ff.; Ezekiel 41:18ff.
39. Ezekiel 47 and Revelation 21 and 22.

issuing forth of the river, which in both passages flows on a fructifying course eastward. Ezekiel sees the river emerging from under the lintel of the temple entrance, which, as we have seen, was a reflex in the temple's architectural symbolism of the Glory-cloud, whose mountain throne-site in Eden was evidently the spring-source of the river of paradise.[40]

Thus, in producing the tabernacle as a symbolic image of his Glory-Spirit, the Creator Lord so designed it that it also recapitulated the macrocosmic and microcosmic versions of the Glory-temple which he fashioned in the original creation. And as God crowned the finished Genesis creation with his majestic Glory over Eden, so, when the tabernacle stood complete at Sinai, the Glory-cloud covered and filled it, sealing it as an authentic likeness of the Spirit-temple (Exod. 40:34ff.), the Alpha and Omega of all creation.

Aaron's Robes—A Replica of the Glory-Tabernacle

In the broad parallelism that we have traced between the Genesis and Exodus creation episodes, Aaron's priestly investiture corresponds to the original creation of man in the image of God's Glory. The priestly vestments had the Glory-cloud for a pattern. This becomes readily apparent once we have recognized that the tabernacle too was a replica of the Glory-cloud, for there are striking similarities between the tabernacle and the priestly vestments. These similarities are made all the more conspicuous in the Book of Exodus by the immediate jux-taposition there of the description of the tabernacle itself (Exod. 25–27) and the instructions for the holy garments of those who minis-tered in the tabernacle (Exod. 28). The tabernacle thus serves as an intermediate link in a remarkable symbolic series: the tabernacle is a replica of the Glory-Spirit and Aaron's vestments are a replica of the tabernacle—and thus also of the Glory-Spirit.

That Aaron's garments were designed to be a likeness of the earthly tabernacle and of the heavenly Glory-tabernacle is evidenced by their materials, form, function, general purpose, and the ritual connected with them. The opening statement about their purpose in Exodus 28:2

---

40. All of this appears again in the New Testament version (Rev. 21 and 22).

alerts us at once to their similarity to the Glory theophany. They were designed "for glory (*kāḇôḏ*) and for beauty *tip'ereṯ*)." The same words appear at the conclusion of the prescriptions for these garments in Exodus 28:40 (cf. Exod. 39:28). Like *kāḇôḏ*, the term *tip'ereṯ* is used for the Glory theophany[41] and for the throne-site where the Glory abides, whether heavenly or earthly sanctuary or ark.[42] Moses and Aaron, worshiping at God's footstool, where he spoke to them from the pillar of cloud,[43] must be provided with such glory-beauty, for those who minister in the presence of the Glory of the Lord must reflect his holy beauty.[44] Moses' transfigured countenance was his glory-reflection, but for Aaron the holy vestments were appointed as a symbolic equivalent, imaging the Glory-beauty of the fiery Shekinah. It was in Aaron's holy turban, which is denoted by a noun formation (*(pe'ēr)* of the same root as *tip'ereṯ*,[45] that the character of his vestments as glory-beauty came to crowning expression.

Contributing to the impression of radiance was the flame-colored linen material prescribed for the ephod, with its band and breast-piece, and for the bottom of the robe of the ephod—a shimmering blend of bright reds and blues with the metallic glint of threads of gold.[46] Highlighting the fiery effect were the rings and the braided chains of gold, the radiant golden crown of the mitre, and the gleam of precious stones set in gold on the shoulder straps of the ephod and the breast-piece.[47] Artist could scarcely do more with an earthly palette in a cold medium to produce the effect of fiery light.

The flame-hued linen of the priestly garments evidenced the fact that they were a scaled-down version of the tabernacle, as well as a symbol

---

41. Isaiah 28:5f.; 60:19; 63:12-15; cf. I Chronicles 29:11, 13; Psalms 71:8; 89:17 (18).
42. I Chronicles 22:5; II Chronicles 3:6; Psalms 78:61; 96:6; Isaiah 60:7.
43. Psalm 99:6, 7.
44. I Chronicles 16:29; Psalm 110:3.
45. Exodus 39:28; Ezekiel 44:18.
46. The interpretation of the ephod as a reflective image of God's heavenly robe of flame finds support in the use of '*ᵃp̄uddāh* for the sheathing of an idol image (Isa. 30:22; cf. Exod. 28:8; 39:5). Of interest in this general connection is the Homeric motif of a goddess endowing a hero, particularly about the shoulders and head, with golden storm cloud and flaming glory.
47. Compare the stones of fire of the Glory that crowns the holy mount (Ezek. 28:13f.). See note 5 above.

of the Glory itself. For this fabric was of a piece with the inside curtains of the tabernacle and with the material of its entrance screen and the inner veil before the ark.[48] In the tabernacle, too, gold was used, with silver and bronze, to heighten the expression of glory.

Like the tabernacle and the theophanic cloud-formation, the priestly vestments were multilayered coverings. The order of the heavenly cloud strata, from inside to outside, which was duplicated in the sanctuary coverings, was reversed in the priests' garments. For whereas the Glory was stationed within the tabernacle, it was external to the priest so that it was his outer garments that directly reflected the light of the Glory standing over against him. Thus, the inner priestly garments (like the tunic) corresponded to the outer skin-coverings of the tabernacle. Then, over the tunic was the robe, a firmament of blue,[49] and over it was the ephod, the direct refulgence of the effulgence of the Glory, and thus an equivalent of the inmost tabernacle curtains that reflected back the Shekinah light within the holy of holies.

A certain similarity in form between the sacred clothing and the sacred tent would be a natural concomitant of the covering function they had in common. But the tent-styling of the garments seems to be accentuated. Thus, the seamless robe is clearly a scaled-down tent. So also is the ephod, made of front and back flaps connected by straps over the shoulder ridge. Possibly the arrangement of golden cords by which the breast-piece was fastened down to golden rings in the ephod was meant to bring to mind tent pegs and cords.

Also discernible in the shoulder pieces of the ephod viewed together with the priestly turban-crown is the motif of the gate of heaven with name-banner lintel, which (as observed above) was one facet of the symbolic meaning of the Glory formation and came to expression too in various ways in the tabernacle and temple. One interesting indication of this is the biblical usage, peculiar to tabernacle and temple architecture, whereby the two side-posts of entryways are called "shoulders," the first occurrence being just before the directions for the priests' garments.[50] This usage of "shoulder" is immediately as-

---

48. Exodus 26:1ff.
49. For a similar tabernacle covering see Numbers 4:6ff.
50. Exodus 27:14, 15. Cf. I Kings 6:8, 7:39; II Kings 11:11; Ezekiel 40:18, 40ff.; 41:2, 26; 46:19; 47:1, 2.

sociated with *mipṭān*, "lintel," in Ezekiel 47:1, 2. While the shoulder pieces of the ephod represented the "shoulders" of the entry-gate, the priestly headdress formed the lintel name-banner. This is suggested both by its lintel-like position between and above the shoulder pieces and by the fact that it bore the name of God in the inscription of its golden plate: "holy to Yahweh."[51]

It may well be that the breast-piece fastened on the front face of the ephod[52] was intended to be an equivalent of the holy of holies. Since what is outmost in the vestments corresponds to what is inmost in the tabernacle, the position of the breast-piece is suitable. Moreover, it was made of the same gold and flame-colored material as the holy of holies and its square shape corresponded at once to the square frame of the entrance to the holy of holies[53] and to all the square faces of that cuboid room. And functionally the breast-piece was, like the holy of holies, the locus of the divine judgment oracle, being called "the breast-piece of judgment" (Exod. 28:15).[54]

To the structural and functional parallels between the vestments and the tabernacle may be added the similarity of ritual treatment accorded them. When they were made and in readiness, the tabernacle erected and the garments arrayed on Aaron and his sons, they were alike consecrated to God by pouring on them the same special oil.[55] As Psalm 133:2 pictures it, the oil poured copiously on Aaron's holy mitre flowed down over the rest of his vestments. By this saturating anointing with the golden symbol of the Spirit of glory and life, the tabernacle and vestments were impregnated with the likeness of God. In the figure of Aaron, clothed in Glory-like vestments and anointed with the holy oil,[56] a double symbol of the Glory-Spirit stands before us.

---

51. Engraved on precious stones on the shoulder pieces (the side-pillars in the entry imagery) were the names of the sons of Israel (Exod. 28:9ff.). Note that the incarnate Glory promises that his people will be made pillars in God's temple, bearing the name of God and the holy city and the Lord's own new name (Rev. 3:12; cf. I Tim. 3:15).
52. Exodus 28:15ff.
53. Compare the main temple entrance (Ezek. 41:21).
54. If the Urim and Thummim, the oracular articles deposited in the breast-piece, were symbolic analogues of the covenant tablets deposited in the ark, an equivalence of the breast-piece and the ark (which was square on the sides) might be possible.
55. Exodus 28:41; 29:5-9; 30:23-30; 40:9-15.
56. Exodus 28:41.

What was thus portrayed by the holy anointing was afterwards manifested in the reality of the descent of the Glory-cloud itself on the
tabernacle, covering and filling it.[57] Similarly, the Spirit is spoken of
as coming upon and filling men.[58] Most significant for our understanding of priestly clothing as a symbol of the Glory-Spirit is the fact that
the Spirit is said to ''clothe'' (literally) a man when he comes upon him
bringing him into a condition of pneumatic likeness to himself in wisdom
and power (Judg. 6:34; I Chron. 12:18[19]; II Chron. 24:20).[59]

One further point of correspondence will suffice in substantiation of
the symbolic equivalence of the priestly garments and the tabernacle.
Common to the ritual treatment of both was a sabbatical pattern. The
holy garments were to be worn in a consecration ritual lasting seven
days.[60] Similarly, the dedication of the tabernacle altar was a seven-
day process.[61]

With this seven-day pattern we come back to our earlier observation
that the record to which the account of the tabernacle and Aaron's
tabernacle-vestments belongs portrays the exodus-covenant event as a
process of re-creation. In this re-creation process the tabernacle corresponds to the original cosmos-temple as a kingdom-temple made after
the pattern of the Glory-temple and Aaron's investiture recalls the
Genesis 1 episode of the creation of man in the likeness of the Glory-
Spirit as the personal image-temple of God.[62]

Illuminated by this symbolic redemptive version, creation in the
image of God is found to signify appointment to holy office with
Spirit-endowment of God-like glory and judicial commission to discern between good and evil. For the ritual of Aaron's investiture and
anointing was an ordination to priesthood, a placing of the government

---

57. Exodus 40:34; cf. I Kings 8:10, 11.
58. See, for example, Exodus 31:2ff.
59. Cf. I Kings 19:13, 19; II Kings 2:8, 13f. Note also the correspondence between the
episodes in II Chronicles 24:20f. and Acts 7:51ff. (especially v. 55).
60. Exodus 29:30, 35.
61. For the sabbatical pattern in the building and erection of the temple see I Kings
6:38; 8:65; II Chronicles 7:8, 9.
62. Aaron's investiture-consecration was a sabbatical creation in which the original
Sabbath, hallowed to the Lord, was matched by the crowning item of the priest's
adornment, the mitre with its signet-seal proclaiming his sanctification to the Lord. Cf.
Psalm 106:16 and Isaiah 58:13.

upon his shoulders and a filling of his hands with the keys of judicial authority.[63] It will be seen that the biblical concepts of image of God and messiah are very much the same.

Glory-Investiture in the New Testament

It is in the tabernacle-fashioning of Aaron's priestly garments that the explanation is found for Paul's curiously mixed metaphor of clothing-building noted at the outset of the chapter. The apostle's use of the priestly investiture figure to expound the idea of our renewal in the image of God[64] corroborates the identification of Aaron's investiture in glory robes as a counterpart to the creation of man in the image of God in Genesis 1 and thereby affords further biblical confirmation of the interpretation of the image of God as a likeness to the divine Glory, a likeness consisting in the glory of a priest's righteous juridical dominion and holy refulgence of the divine light.

In a Pauline variation of the metaphor of putting on the priestly vestments as a symbol of image renewal, those vestments become the armor of God.[65] Part of the inspiration for this figure is Isaiah 61:10c and d, where God is said to clothe his people with the garments of salvation and robes of righteousness. From Isaiah 59:17ff. it appears that the prophet was thinking in terms of a warrior's garments. The latter passage also shows that for the prophet, too, clothing people with salvation was a matter of producing in them a likeness to God. For God himself is there described as putting on righteousness as his armor and salvation as a helmet on his head (Isa. 59:17a) as he comes, a divine warrior, in his Glory for judgment.[66] It is particularly to be noticed how Paul's reference to the helmet of salvation among the items of Christian armor (Eph. 6:17 and I Thess. 5:8) is accounted for by the terminology of the combined contexts of Isaiah 59 and 61 (especially 59:17 and 61:10). The Isaianic source of Paul's metaphor not only shows that the armor is indeed a variation of the clothing figure used

---

63. See Isaiah 22:21-24 for the imagery of induction to office by enrobing. For priestly pronouncements in terms of cultic good and evil see Leviticus 27:12, 14.
64. See. p. 35.
65. Romans 13:12, 14; Ephesians 6:11ff.; I Thessalonians 5:8.
66. Compare verses 17b–19.

elsewhere by the apostle for the image-of-God idea, but it identifies
this clothing as priestly in character. In comparing the act of clothing
to a bridegroom's arraying of himself for the wedding, Isaiah uses a
denominative of the word *priest,* meaning literally ''to act as a priest''
(Isa. 61:10e). Agreeably, some of the pieces of equipment that Paul
lists in the Christian armor correspond to prominent items in the
priestly vestments, such as the breast-piece and sash. Moreover, this
armor is designed for the function of guarding what is holy against the
attacks of the devil (Eph. 6:11ff.) and that is a distinctly priestly task.
Items of Christian armor such as the shield and sword reflect directly
features and functions of the divine Glory, while the fiery radiance of
that Glory is reflected in the characterization of the Christian armor in
general as the armor of light (Rom. 13:12).

It was observed in the first chapter[67] that the Book of Revelation
opens with a vision of Christ as the archetypal Glory-Spirit-temple and
closes with a vision of the church re-created by Christ in his glory-
image and thus an ectypal temple in the Spirit. Supplementing that, we
may now draw attention to the use of the symbolism of priestly investiture in this Apocalyptic treatment of the theme of re-creation in the
divine image. The symbolism of investiture in the Glory-covering is
used in this instance not for the individual believer's experience but for
the corporate renewal of the church as the new man in the image of
God.

Christ appears in the opening vision of Revelation as an incarnate
Glory-Spirit, but the figure seen by John is also the antitype of Aaron
invested with the holy garments emblematic of the divine Glory. The
priestly nature of the figure is indicated by his location: he stands in the
midst of the seven golden lampstands of the sanctuary (Rev. 1:12, 13).
He is a royal priest with the keys of office received by holy ordination,
with authority to open and close (Rev. 1:18; 3:7; cf. Isa. 22:22). The
first thing described is his clothing (Rev. 1:13b) and the term used for
his long robe (found only here in the New Testament) is used in the
Septuagint for the high priest's robe and ephod and its breast-piece,
while the golden sash recalls the sash of the ephod made of the flame-
colored material interwoven with threads of gold. The coalescence of

67. See pp. 24ff.

A PRIESTLY MODEL OF THE IMAGE OF GOD   49

the symbolism of the priestly vestments with the Glory-cloud in this vision of Christ is another clear biblical exposition of the symbolic meaning of Aaron's robes as an image of the Glory-Spirit.

The church as portrayed in Revelation 21 and 22 is a church re-created in the likeness of Christ, the Glory-robed priest of Revelation 1. Coupled in this portrait with the symbol of the temple-city, New Jerusalem, is the symbol of the "bride *adorned* for her husband" (Rev. 21:2). Here again is the combination of the figures of clothing and building which we have traced back to the tabernacle-vestments that adorned Aaron the high priest. And, on examination, the bridal adornment of Revelation 21 is indeed found to consist of priestly vestments made after the pattern of the robes of the church's bridegroom-Lord depicted in Revelation 1.

In Revelation 19:7-9, in a preliminary reference to the church-bride prepared for the marriage of the Lamb, she is described as arrayed in the fine linen repeatedly insisted on for the priests' clothing[68] and representing the "righteousness of saints."[69] Those so arrayed are described in Revelation 7:15 as continually engaged in the priestly service of God in his temple. Certain features of Aaron's holy vestments appear in the picture of the tabernacle-city in Revelation 21 and since the bride is identified with this city, urban adornment is here interchangeable with bridal adornment.[70] Such features are the lavish use of gold, the square shape,[71] and especially the twelve precious stones constituting the foundations of the wall and bearing the names of the covenant people.[72] The curious way in which details of the priestly vestments are thus interwoven in the adornment of the bride-priest and the tabernacle-city is itself a further confirmation of the interpretation of Aaron's vestments as a sartorial copy of the tabernacle structure.

---

68. Exodus 28 and 29.
69. Cf. Revelation 6:11; 7:14.
70. Revelation 21:2, 9, 10. In Revelation 18:16 the same mixed figure is used for the city of Babylon.
71. Compare the breast-piece of the ephod.
72. In the case of the bride-city the names are those of the apostles, the names of the twelve tribes having been allocated to the gates of the city. Of interest for the total complex of relationships being traced in the present studies is the appearance of most of the twelve stones of the breast-piece of judgment as a covering in Eden, the garden of God (Ezek. 28:13).

An Old Testament version of the consummation prospects presented in the Book of Revelation can be found in the closing chapters of Isaiah. With regard to the particular symbolism we are dealing with, Isaiah 62 occupies an intermediate position in the biblical trajectory between the priestly prescriptions of Exodus and the Book of Revelation. The prophet has just spoken of the Spirit of the Lord's transformation of Zion through the messianic Servant into a thing of beauty, joy, and glory (Isa. 61:1-3). The people of Jerusalem will be priests of the Lord, ministers of God (Isa. 61:6). It is to this context too, along with Isaiah 59, that we have traced the Christian armor figure, noting that Isaiah likens the salvation investiture to the adorning of a bridegroom-priest (Isa. 61:10e). We may now further note that this investiture is likened to the adorning of the bride (Isa. 61:10f). This marriage figure is resumed in Isaiah 62 and there, as in Revelation 21, is found the double symbol of the city-wife, Jerusalem-Hephzibah, over whom God will rejoice as a bridegroom rejoices over his bride (vv. 4, 5). This bride-city is characterized by radiant "glory" and "beauty" (vv. 1-3), the same terms as are used for the holy garments of the priest and for the Glory theophany.[73]

Another Old Testament passage on which Revelation 21 is dependent is Ezekiel 16. Here in a metaphorical treatment of the exodus history, Israel is a bride adorned in garments whose identification with the tabernacle covering is unmistakable. We shall return to this passage presently but simply call attention to it here as a further important source of support for our interpretation of the bridal adornment of Revelation 21. Our conclusion is then that the church-bride of Revelation 21 is portrayed as a priest figure, arrayed in holy tabernacle-vestments of glory. Thus, the Book of Revelation, in making its symbolic statement that the church glorified is a church renewed in the image of God revealed in Christ,[74] equates this image renewal with a priestly investiture in the Glory of God.

Image-Investiture and Covenant

In the remarkable historical allegory of Ezekiel 16, Israel in the wilderness is a woman at the age of love, with whom the Lord enters

73. Cf. Deuteronomy 26:19; Jeremiah 13:11.
74. Revelation 1:13ff.

into covenant, taking her as his wife.[75] As a token of the marriage
covenant he spreads the corner of his robe (*kānāp*) over her (v. 8), a
ritual indicative of a man's bringing a woman under his protection.[76]
The allusion of this nuptial imagery is to God's sheltering of Israel
under the Glory-cloud. "He spread a cloud for a covering; and fire to
give light in the night" (Ps. 105:39). The psalmist here uses the same
verb (*pāraš*) with reference to the spreading of the theophanic cloud-
canopy as is used in Ezekiel 16:8 for God's extending the edge of his
robe. Another detail in this verse that evokes the Glory-cloud is the
designation of the hem of the robe by the term *kānāp*, "wing, extrem-
ity," for wings are often associated with the Glory-cloud, particularly
in figurative descriptions of God's protective overshadowing of his
people.[77] According to Ezekiel's allegorical transcription of the Sinaitic covenant-making, the covering of Israel by the theophanic Presence
was a divine plighting of troth.[78] The posture of the Glory-Spirit on
Mount Sinai was an oath stance, signifying covenant ratification.

Parenthetically, we may mention the related symbolic act of taking
hold of the hem of a robe, employed in the ancient world as an expression of importunate supplication[79] or in acknowledgment of submis-
sion, specifically, in covenantal commitment.[80] Perhaps this broader
covenantal usage was a secondary development reflecting the nuptial
covenanting signified by covering with the skirt. The covenantal significance of the hem of the garment was utilized and enhanced in the
requirement of the Mosaic covenants that the Israelites put tassels with
a cord of blue on the four corners of their robes as a reminder of their
covenantal obligations.[81] In the formulation of this requirement, God's
covenant with Israel is viewed as a marriage, for what the tassels are
designed to avoid is religious adultery.[82] A comparable covenantal

---

75. Cf. Jeremiah 2:2.
76. For the custom, see Ruth 3:9. Cf. Deuteronomy 22:30; 27:20.
77. In I Kings 8:7 *pāraš* is used for the spreading of the wings of the cherubim over the
ark.
78. See note 24 above.
79. Zechariah 8:23; Matthew 9:20; 14:36.
80. Cf. R. A. Brauner, "'To Grasp the Hem' and I Samuel 15:27," *The Journal of
the Ancient Near Eastern Society of Columbia University* 6 (1974): 35-38. On the
important role of garments in covenant-making at Mari and Alalakh, see D. J. Wise-
man, "Abban and Alalakh," *Journal of Cuneiform Studies* 12 (1958): 129.
81. Numbers 15:38, 39a; Deuteronomy 22:12.
82. Numbers 15:39b. Note laws of adultery following Deuteronomy 22:12.

function was performed by the golden tassel-like "bells" suspended from the bottom of the high priest's robes, which evidently served as a reminder to the Lord so that, hearing their metallic jingle as the high priest approached, he would remember his covenanted mercy and the priest would not perish in his presence.[83]

Having depicted the covering of Israel by the Glory-cloud as a spreading of God's garment over his bride-people and thus as a token of covenantal engagement, Ezekiel's allegory continues with the sealing of the Sinaitic Covenant by the setting up of God's holy tent, his entrance into it, and his reception there of Israel in the person of Aaron the high priest as his bride-people. This consummation of the covenant at Sinai is portrayed in the allegory as an act of investiture, an adorning of the bride in her wedding garments. And these garments are described in terms that recall the tabernacle and Aaron's tabernacle-vestments, the replicas of God's Glory-robe.[84]

As the allegory pictures it, Yahweh found the woman Israel destitute and naked (Ezek. 16:6, 7). But entering by oath into a marriage covenant with her (v. 8), he washed and anointed her (v. 9), then adorned her in the perfection of beauty from head to foot (vv. 10-14). Her clothing was of fine linen with embroidered work, like the material of the tabernacle and Aaron's robes.[85] The bridal adornment was like them too in its inclusion of gold and silver and gems. The bridal crown recalls Aaron's holy crown. A more subtle allusion to the tabernacle is the tahaš-skin[86] of the bride's sandals, a material mentioned elsewhere in the Old Testament only with reference to the outer skin-covering of the sacred tent. The washing and anointing of the bride (v. 9) corre-

---

83. Exodus 28:33ff.; 39:25f. Incidentally, this identifying sound of the "wing" of the priestly robe echoed the Glory-chariot, for it too had a characteristic heralding sound, explained by Ezekiel in terms of the wings of the cherubim (Ezek. 1:24; 3:13). In the architecture of Ezekiel's apocalyptic temple, a feature corresponding to the alternating pomegranates and tassel-bells of the high priest's robes is seen in the alternating palm trees and cherubim carved along the bottom "skirt" of the walls (Ezek. 41:17ff.). Suspended pomegranates are also found as a decorative feature under the rim of a circular bronze pedestal at Ras Shamra. On the sound of the theophany see further chapter four.

84. Cf. Psalm 104:1, 2.

85. Biblical references to embroidered work are largely concentrated in the prescriptions for the tabernacle and Aaron's vestments. See Exodus 26:36; 27:16; 28:39; 35:35; 36:37; 38:18, 23; 39:29.

86. The identity of the tahaš is uncertain.

spond to the ritual procedures for the investiture and ordination of the priests.[87] There is also a reference to the priestly service in what is said of the bride's provisions of the fine flour and oil (v. 13). The cultic allusion of this is borne out as the allegory continues (vv. 15ff.) and the bride turned harlot is described in deallegorized terms as devoting her bridal provisions to the service of idol cults.[88]

According to Ezekiel's interpretation, God's spreading of his Glory-cloud as a canopy over Israel, the equivalent action of setting up his tabernacle to receive Israel in her priesthood under its covering, and the further equivalent of clothing Israel's priests with the glory vestments all signified God's ratification of his covenant with Israel. In the marriage covenant of the allegory, the two main moments in the divine procedure are acts involving clothing, with the pledge signified by the first act fulfilled in the second. The Lord takes his bride-people into covenantal union by the promissory act of spreading his robe of Glory over her and then by clothing her in garments fashioned after the pattern of his Glory-robe, so that she stands before him transformed into the image of his Glory. Thus ingeniously the prophetic parable interweaves the concepts of the covenant and the image of God, revealing their mutuality by covering them both under the one symbol of investiture in the divine Glory.[89]

The same correlation of re-creation in the image of God and covenant consummation obtains in the other contexts we have examined in Isaiah and the Book of Revelation which use the model of priestly-bridal investiture in God-like glory.

Further evidence of the correlation of covenant and image of God is found in a concept that interlocks with them both, the concept of bearing God's name as a surname. This name-bearing theme overlaps the whole range of ideas found in the meaning-field of the image-of-God concept. The archetypal Glory is identified as the Name of Yahweh. Thus, with reference to the Shekinah-Presence in the sanctuary, God is said to have put his Name there[90] or caused his Name

---

87. Exodus 29:4ff.; 40:12ff.
88. Cf. Jeremiah 2:32.
89. A similar blend of motifs is found in the messianic marriage allegory of Psalm 45.
90. Deuteronomy 12:5, 21; 14:24. See above the discussion of the Glory as name-banner.

to dwell there.[91] Similarly, God's Name is said to have been in the Angel of the Presence.[92] God's Name is God in theophanic revelation. The tabernacle-temple replicas of the Glory theophany bear the name of God,[93] and the tabernacle-vested priest bears the name of Yahweh on his head. The idea is that these persons and things are holy. They are consecrated to God who acknowledges them as peculiarly his own. Likewise, men and angels as offspring-images of God their Father have a divine patronymic; they are named "sons of God,"[94] just as peoples customarily are surnamed after the name of their forebears.[95]

The equivalence of the bearing of God's name and the bearing of God's image appears strikingly in Revelation 22:4. Here, in the midst of the description of the glorified covenant community, renewed after the image of the Lord, it is said: "They will see his face and his name will be in their foreheads." This marks the fulfillment of Christ's promise to incorporate the overcomer in his temple as a pillar and to "write on him the name of my God, and the name of the city of my God, the New Jerusalem which comes down out of heaven from my God, and my new name" (Rev. 3:12).[96] The church's bearing of Christ's new name is exponential of its new nature as the new city-temple, the priest-bride arrayed in tabernacle-glory, the image of the Glory-Spirit-Lord, the glory of the bridegroom-Son. Behind the imagery of Revelation 22:4 are the figures of Moses and Aaron. Aaron bore on his forehead the name of the Lord inscribed on the crown on the front of the priestly mitre. The very countenance of Moses was transfigured into a reflective likeness of the Glory-Face, the Presence-Name of God, when God talked with him "mouth to mouth" (Num. 12:8) out of the Glory-cloud.[97] As the Name and the Glory are alike designations of the Presence of God in the theophanic cloud, so both name and glory describe the reflected likeness of God. To say that the overcomers in the New Jerusalem bear the name of Christ on their forehead is to

---

91. Deuteronomy 12:11; 14:23; 16:2, 6, 11; 26:2.
92. Exodus 23:21.
93. I Kings 8:43; cf. II Samuel 6:2; I Chronicles 13:6; Ezekiel 48:35.
94. Cf. Ephesians 3:15.
95. Cf. Genesis 21:12; 48:5, 6; Isaiah 44:5; 48:1.
96. Cf. note 51 above. See also Revelation 2:17; 14:1; 19:12f.
97. Cf. note 22 above.

say that they reflect the glory of Christ, which is to say that they bear the image of the glorified Christ.

The theme of God's name is equally conspicuous in the biblical treatment of God's covenants. In their treaty formulation, covenants are introduced as a revelation of God's name. Also, in both Old and New Testaments the people of the covenant are those who are called by God's name and thus identified as his children or people under the authority of his rule.[98] The New Testament disciples were called "Christians"[99] and the force of the form *christianos* is that those who bear the name of Christ belong to Christ, as servants to a lord.[100] The name "Christian" is a covenantal identification for the servant-son people of the new covenant. A characteristic action of God's people is denoted by an active equivalent of the expression "to be called by the name of." Usually translated "call on the name of the Lord," the phrase is at times to be rendered "confess the name of the Lord."[101] The significance of this confessing of God's name is to acknowledge the covenant Lord as Creator-Father, to claim his name as surname.[102]

Discovery of the biblical nexus between the concepts of image of God and divine covenant validates Covenant Theology's identification of the Creator's relation to man at the beginning as a covenantal arrangement.[103] In the light of the interrelation we have found between covenant and image of God, the fact of man's creation in God's image, explicitly affirmed in Genesis 1:27, would in and of itself signify the existence of a covenant. But there is the further fact, observed above, that the Glory-Spirit, who was the creative Archetype of man's ectypal glory-likeness, was present as a crowning and sheltering canopy over man in Eden. This tells us again that we are to construe the creation order as a covenant order. For according to the analogy of Scripture, God's covering of his people with his Glory, which is associated with

---

98. Deuteronomy 28:10; Psalms 89:24-28 (25-29); Isaiah 43:6, 7; 63:8, 15, 16, 19; cf. Isaiah 65:1; Zechariah 13:9.

99. Acts 11:26; cf. Isaiah 65:15.

100. Cf. E. J. Bickerman, "The Name of Christians," *Harvard Theological Review* 42, 2 (1949): 118f.

101. For example, Genesis 4:26; Psalm 105:1; Isaiah 64:7, 8; cf. Romans 15:20; Ephesians 1:21; II Timothy 2:19.

102. Isaiah 44:5.

103. Cf. my *By Oath Consigned* (Grand Rapids: Eerdmans, 1968), pp. 26ff.

his investiture of them with his image, is an act of covenantal engagement.[104]

Here, in the record of the Covenant of Creation, is the ultimate source of the combination of elements found in the allegory of Ezekiel 16: the divine covenantal covering, the tabernacle-investiture of man as image of God, and the marriage covenant.[105] In Genesis 2, marriage covenant is present explicitly in the form of a societal analogue to mankind's covenantal-image relationship to God. Through the parable of the marriage relationship of the man and the woman, established by creation ordinance, instructive insight was afforded into the nature of the covenant between God and men. The woman-wife, derived from the man as bone of his bone and flesh of his flesh, was the image-likeness of the man. The name-pun brings this out: She was called 'iššāh, "woman," because she was taken from 'iš "man," (Gen. 2:23). And the man-husband received the woman, his image, in a covenant of marriage (Gen. 2:22-24),[106] under his lordship, to bear his name,[107] and to be his glory,[108] not least by bearing him image-sons to fill the earth with his name.

The parable of human marriage-covenant was fully exploited in the revelation of redemptive re-creation and covenant. The church-bride, derived from Christ, the second Adam, as glory of his Glory and spirit of his Spirit, is a re-creation in his image. As a likeness of derivation, like that of the woman in relation to the man (and the son in relation to his father), the glory-image of the church-bride is possessed under the authority of her husband-Lord. Christ takes his church, his image-wife, in covenant of marriage to bear his glory and his name, to be the fulness of him who fills all in all.[109]

---

104. In chapter one above, p. 19, it was observed that the appearance of the Glory in oath-stance over creation, referred to in Genesis 1:2, imparted a covenantal character to the event.
105. For the earliest roots of this imagery in redemptive history see Genesis 3:21.
106. Cf. Proverbs 2:17; Malachi 2:14.
107. Cf. Isaiah 4:1.
108. I Corinthians 11:3, 7.
109. Ephesians 1:23; cf. Psalm 45:16, 17 (17, 18).

Chapter Three

A Prophetic Model of the Image of God

When we analyze the forming and functioning of the Old Testament prophets, we discover that the distinctive traits of prophethood coincide with the features we have found to constitute the *imago Dei*. As we read the history and writings of the prophets we see the Spirit creatively active in their lives, replicating his Glory-likeness in them. To perceive the prophetic experience as an instance of creation in the image of God sheds light on the nature and purpose of the prophetic office. But our immediate interest here is to see how the biblical concept of the *imago Dei* is clarified as it is given tangible substance, embodied in the prophets.

That there is a prophetic model of the image of God in the Scriptures alongside the model of priestly investiture is, then, what we wish to point out in this chapter. We shall start with an analysis of the nature of the prophetic office, noting the correspondence between its components and those of the *imago Dei*. Then we shall focus on the mediator theme of the Old Testament story of the re-creation of the prophets in the likeness of the Spirit and see how two figures, one human and one divine, played roles in the image creating process that were prototypal of Christ's mediatorial role in the New Testament stage of the image story. And finally we shall examine some biblical passages whose theme is the re-creation of God's people in the Glory-likeness and show how they make use of the prophetic model of the *imago Dei*.

The Prophet as Image of the Glory-Spirit

Adam's creation as image-reflector of the glory of the Creator-Spirit was recapitulated in the history of the prophets. The critical event in the formation of a prophet was a transforming encounter with the

Glory-Spirit from which the prophet emerged as a man reflecting the divine Glory. Scripture describes this creative act of the Spirit by a variety of verbs. Among these are verbs to rest or fall on, to take hold of, to lift up, to bring here or there, to enter into, to fill, and to invest.[1] As thus acted upon by the Spirit, the prophet was so Spirit-conditioned that "man of the Spirit" could serve as a synonym for "prophet."[2]

To be caught up in the Spirit was to be received into the divine assembly, the heavenly reality within the theophanic Glory-Spirit.[3] The hallmark of the true prophet was that he had stood before the Lord of Glory in the midst of this deliberative council of angels, while the false prophet was one who had not done so and consequently lacked divine legitimation and essential qualification.[4] It was by such a vision-rapture into the heavenly Presence that the prophets' call came to them, raising them up for their mission as plenipotentiary emissaries of the Lord of hosts, who was enthroned in the heavenly court. Such was the call that came to an Isaiah[5] or Ezekiel.[6] Introduced into the council, privileged to hear there the disclosure of the Lord's purposes, the prophets were ready to be sent to men on earth as authoritative spokesmen, as the very mouth of God.[7]

By virtue of his Spirit-rapture into heaven the prophet took on the glory that diffused the heavenly court. He was transformed into the likeness of the King of Glory whom he beheld there on his throne high and lifted up, the train of his Glory-robe filling the royal temple.

In becoming a participant of the divine council and a reflector of the Glory of the council's King, the prophet also became like the myriad angel members of the council, those "sons of God" who bore the image of their Creator-Lord. One indication that the prophets acquired a likeness to the heavenly beings who belonged to God's council is the fact that a designation of the latter, mal'āk ("angel, messenger"), was

---

1. Use of the verb lāḇaš, "clothe" (II Chron. 24:20) is of particular interest in view of the imagery of investiture with the image of God.
2. Cf. Hosea 9:7.
3. See pp. 17f.
4. Cf. Jeremiah 23:18.
5. Cf. Isaiah 6.
6. Cf. Ezekiel 1-3.
7. Cf. 1 Kings 8:15; II Chronicles 36:22; Isaiah 30:2.

given to prophets.[8] Earlier we observed that likeness to the angels of
the Glory council was involved in man's original creation in the image
of God.[9] We noted that the fiat statement concerning man as image of
God in Genesis 1:26 is linked to the episode of Isaiah's call to prophethood in Isaiah 6 by the plural form of address that is idiomatic in the
divine council.[10] But beyond the common council setting and idiom
shared by those two episodes, they are also linked by the fundamen-
tally similar nature of the events that transpired on the two occasions.
For the prophet Isaiah as for Adam the heavenly council was a place of
origins; it was the site of creation in the likeness of God and his angels.

The particular aspects of the divine Glory reflected by the prophets
are the same ones we have found to be paramount elsewhere in the
biblical concept of the *imago Dei*—judicial, ethical, and physical
glory.

Members of the council played an administrative-judicial role,
whether through participation in the deliberative, juridical session of
the council or in subsequent missions in which they served as authoritative messengers or executors of the decrees of the council. These
functions were an exercise of authority reflective of the sovereign glory
of the One seated on the throne. For the prophets, this governmental-
judicial council activity assumed the form of a covenant mediatorship
like that of Moses. Deuteronomy 18:15-22, the provision for the prophetic office in Israel's treaty-constitution, points back to the role
performed by Moses at the Sinai covenant-making as the paradigm (vv.
16, 17) and forward to the continuation of that function by those whom
God would raise up like unto Moses (vv. 15, 18f.). Moses' authoritative
administration of God's covenant lordship over Israel was to be carried
on by the prophets.[11] In their effective judicial declaration of the
covenant sanctions that God purposed to visit upon his people, the
prophets were engaged in a constructive shaping of the kingdom-house
of God. Similarly in the extension of their mission beyond Israel, the
prophets were appointed over nations and kingdoms to build up and to

---

8. Cf. II Chronicles 36:15,16; Haggai 1:13; Malachi 3:1.
9. See p. 27.
10. See p. 23.
11. The fact that the offices of judge and prophet were combinable, as in Deborah and
Samuel, is indicative of the governmental dimension of the prophetic office.

destroy.[12] Here, in this governing, structuring function of these Moses-like agents of the divine council is that which corresponds in the experience of the prophets to the royal functional aspect of the *imago Dei* as it was bestowed on man at the beginning.[13] The investment of the prophet with heavenly authority to shape the historical course of the kingdom of God in the midst of the kingdoms on earth in the name of the royal Lord of the council was a renewal of the original assignment to man of a God-like dominion over the world, adapted now, of course, to the redemptive situation. It was an act of re-creation in the glory-image of God.

A second element of the *imago Dei* in man's creation endowment was a likeness to the glory of the divine holiness and righteousness.[14] If in his ruling function man was to be a true image of his royal Lord, his exercise of dominion must be informed by those qualities of rectitude and truth that were the very foundation of the throne of God. It was a lie of the tempter to suggest implictly that the absence of the ethical element of the *imago Dei* was irrelevant to the development of man's God-likeness in the area of judicial glory.[15] The truth was that love of the holy will of the heavenly King of kings was essential to man's advancement from glory to glory in his reflection of the glory of the divine majesty.

This same truth meets us again in the story of God's images, the prophets. Before the prophet could be sent as authoritative emissary of God to engage in building God's kingdom he must be ethically qualified. The prerequisite rapture into the divine council involved more than a discovery of the designs and decrees of the council; it included a creative forming of the prophet himself, bringing him into profound inward conformity to the Lord of the council. And there is nothing more remarkable in that image endowment received by the prophets in the Spirit than the way in which their whole being was brought into sympathetic, passionate rapport with God's holy kingdom purpose and its righteous demands and judgments.

In the redemptive production of God-likeness in men, the ethical

---

12. Cf. Jeremiah 1:10; 28:8.
13. See pp. 27 and 31.
14. See footnote 13.
15. Cf. Genesis 3:5.

component of the *imago Dei* becomes more prominent because now the bestowal of this particular glory endowment means facing and finding a way through the crisis posed by the existing obstacle of sin. Within the model of the history of the prophets, Isaiah's account of his call provides a powerful portrayal of this drama of redemptive image renewal. Before he can be commissioned to serve as representative of the council and its King (6:8ff.), the problem of his spiritual disqualification, desperately voiced by Isaiah himself (v. 5), must be addressed. So it happens that the process of fashioning Isaiah in the (special, prophetic) image of God centers in an act of redemptive cleansing (vv. 6, 7).[16] Only so can he be brought into the requisite ethical conformity with the all-holy Lord of hosts (v. 3). Raised up from the midst of unclean mortals, the prophets were in themselves frail, imperfect mortals still. But in their charismatic state as Spirit inspired and enveloped—and thereby renewed after the likeness of the Glory-Spirit—the prophets underwent such spiritual transformation that they could assume a stance over against Israel and the nations as apostles of the divine council and carry out their commission under the constraint of a consuming emotional-ethical sympathy with the holy righteousness and truth of God.

The third feature in our analysis of the biblical concept of the image of God was man's physical mirroring of that luminosity of the Glory theophany which, in a creaturely figure, manifested the pure holy glory of him who is light.[17] As originally created, man was not yet endowed with this form of Glory-likeness. Physical glorification might only be contemplated in eschatological hope. In a variety of ways, however, even this feature is present in the prophetic model of creation in the image of God.

Preeminent among the instances of this is the Sinai experience of the paradigm prophet, Moses. The face-to-face revelation of the Glory-Spirit on the mountain was transfiguring. Moses' own countenance took on a radiance reflective of the light of God's face. In

---

16. An Old Babylonian prayer of a diviner speaks of his performing a ceremony of purification of the mouth in preparation for approach to the assembly of the gods. Cf. Moshe Weinfeld, "Ancient Near Eastern Patterns in Prophetic Literature," *Vetus Testamentum* 27 (1977): 180.
17. See footnote 13.

Exodus 34:29, the verb *qrn*, a denominative of the noun *qeren*, "horn," is used to describe the glowing of Moses' skin. This has an interesting bearing on the correlation of Moses' shining face and the image of God concept. For one thing, in a poetic allusion to God's spectacular procession from the south in the days of Moses, Habakkuk uses the noun *qeren* for the shafts of light radiating from the Glory theophany (3:4). Also, there is the familiar convention of ancient Mesopotamian iconography whereby gods were depicted with horn-crowned heads. In the light of that tradition of symbolic representation we may more fully appreciate the literary figure of Habakkuk 3:4 and Exodus 34:29 and perceive even more clearly the nature of Moses' "horning" countenance as an instance of the replication of the divine Glory.[18]

Moses' shining face was only a partial and passing glorification,[19] but in this phenomenon there was a prophetic intimation of the ultimate resurrection-glorification of God's people in which the *imago Dei* attains full-orbed perfection. Along with this unique instance of Moses' bodily radiance, other astonishing physical phenomena are mentioned in the narratives of Moses and the Moses-like prophets of the Old Testament which also were signs of the eschatological experience of God's image-bearers. There was Elijah's extraordinary passage from place to place[20] and there was the performance of different kinds of miracles by various prophets, none greater in respect to such wonder signs than Moses himself.[21] All such phenomena were so many promissory samples of the powers and capabilities to be enjoyed by those re-created in God's image when, through their physical endowment of glorification, they will have attained to the consummation of their dominion over the creation.

Introduction into the state of glorification will take place by a rapture

---

18. Other formal parallels to the Exodus 34 glory theme in ancient literature point in the same direction. Of interest in this connection is the semantic range of the Akkadian term *melammū*, which denotes both the awesome aureole manifestation of deity and a mask worn by the images of gods or priests. Cf. A. Leo Oppenheim, "Akkadian *pul(u)h(t)u* and *melammu*," *Journal of the American Oriental Society* 63 (1943): 31–34.
19. Cf. II Corinthians 3:7ff.
20. Cf. I Kings 18:12, 46; II Kings 2:16; Ezekiel 3:14; 8:3; Acts 8:39, 40.
21. Cf. Deuteronomy 34:10–12.

of the redeemed into the Glory-cloud.[22] A foretaste of that moment in the process of re-creating the divine image in man was afforded in the rapture of the prophets (whether in the body or out of the body) into the Glory-council. And an earnest of the eschatological rapture was given even more graphically and openly in the bodily translation of the prophet Elijah from this world in the Glory-chariot.[23]

When the creation of man in the divine image is recapitulated in the prophets, it is a redemptive event. The forming of the prophets in God's image belongs to the history of Christ's fashioning of the new man in his likeness. Moreover, it is the ultimate stage of that redemptive renewal of the *imago Dei* that finds portrayal in those transformed men of the Spirit, the prophets. And this means that we can catch a glimpse of our predestined future not in the prophets' visionary, predictive words alone but in their life experience as well. The lives of the prophets caught up in the Spirit were prophecies of the eschatological destiny of mankind re-created in God's image.

The distinctively eschatological quality of the prophets' experience of the divine image is most apparent in the physical dimension of their Glory-likeness because in the regular course of events physical glorification occurs only in the context of the future great day. But it is equally true that the other two aspects of the image of God are exhibited on an eschatological level of glory in the prophetic model. We did indicate earlier the connection of the physical and functional aspects of the prophetic image, noting that the kind of authority over nature and nations given to the prophets was equivalent to the dominion over the world that is achievable only in conjunction with bodily glorification. The ethical aspect of the image in the prophetic model also fits into this pattern. In their Spirit-state the prophets were brought into a sympathetic identity with God tantamount to a "perfect" ethical conformity to God's holiness. Since in the experience of the corporate new man in Christ Jesus[24] attainment of that stage of ethical likeness to God coincides with glorification, this "perfection" of the ethical dimension

---

22. Cf. I Thessalonians 4:17.
23. Cf. II Kings 2:11.
24. Individually, of course, those who have died in the Lord have in that "first resurrection" experience already been blessed with this perfect likeness to the holiness of their Lord.

of the divine image experienced by the prophets in the Spirit had an eschatological character. It is, therefore, the specifically consummated form of the *imago Dei* that is uniformly exhibited in the prophetic model. In raising up these men of the Spirit, God raised up a bright sign of the eschatological glory of all his saints.

Mediators of the Prophetic Image in the Old Testament

In the beginning man was created in the image of God by the power of creative fiat after the paradigm of the theophanic Glory-Spirit. In redemptive history the reproduction of the image of God in the new mankind takes place through the mediatorial agency of Jesus Christ, in whom the divine Glory became incarnate.[25] He is the paradigm of the Glory-image and he is the mediator of the Spirit in the process of replicating the divine likeness. As indicated earlier,[26] the manner in which Christ mediates this renewal of the *imago Dei* is variously depicted, according to the particular way in which he is viewed, whether as Spirit-Lord or as second Adam. Here we want to call attention to the fact that the Old Testament's prophetic model of creation in the Glory image contains anticipatory expressions of this messianic, mediatorial aspect of the impartation of the divine image.[27]

Two such mediatorial agents appear in the history of the prophets. One was Moses.

Moses

Moses was prototypal of Christ in respect to his endowment with the image of the Glory-Spirit. He enjoyed as a continuing privilege access to the Glory-Presence and to the creative encounter in that Presence we have seen was productive of a Glory-likeness in the prophets. Moreover, the revelatory experience granted to Moses was more intimate than that of the prophets, as the Lord himself affirms in the

---

25. Cf. Colossians 2:9.
26. See pp. 28f.
27. Besides the special phase of the history of the *imago Dei* found in the experience of the prophets there is also the general renewing of the divine image in God's people in Old Testament times. This redemptive activity of the Spirit was also proleptically attributable to the later mediatorial accomplishments of Christ.

statement related in Numbers 12:6–8. When God raised up prophets, they experienced the divine self-disclosure in a more visionary state (v. 6). It was otherwise with Moses, whose station was above all the other prophets and all other servants in God's Old Testament house (v. 7). He entered within the cloud-veil in a normal, not ecstatic or dreamlike state, and there spoke with the Lord mouth to mouth (v. 8a)—or, "face to face as a man speaks with his friend" (Exod. 33:11a). He was not limited to hearing the thunderous voice of the Lord, while the form (t*e*mûnāh) of God was hidden from his sight, as was the case with the Israelite people at Sinai.[28] Moses might behold the t*e*mûnāh of God enthroned in the Glory (v. 8c), a prophetic token of what awaits the saints at their resurrection, when they will gaze on God's Face and be enraptured with his t*e*mûnāh (as the blessed hope is expressed in Psalm 17:15).[29]

From his privileged coming before the Glory-Face Moses emerged as God's prophet-servant, endowed in impressive measure with all those features imparted in the Spirit-transformation of the prophets— the features that coincided, as we have seen, with the glory elements constitutive of the *imago Dei*. The official-functional element of the glory image in Moses consisted in his status as the one entrusted with a unique authority over the whole old economy, together with his role as agent of divine judgment on the world kingdoms. The element of ethical glory is seen in that intimate identification of Moses with the

---

28. Cf. Deuteronomy 4:12. Contrast also the revelatory experience claimed by Eliphaz in Job 4:16. This verse presents difficulties but the following translation appears preferable to the usual renderings: "It stood still. I did not see its appearance; its form was not before my eyes. I heard a loud voice." On the last clause, see the discussion of I Kings 19:12 in the next chapter.

29. Possibly the term *mar'eh* in Numbers 12:8b also refers to the privileged view of God enjoyed by Moses in contrast to the prophets. But since *mar'eh* is elsewhere used for the kind of vision received by the prophets and that kind of revelatory experience is, moreover, denoted here in verse 6 by the very similar noun *mar'āh,* another interpretation of verse 8b should be sought. Perhaps the negative (and the preposition) with the following *ḥîḏōṯ* does double duty with *mar'eh*. Such ellipsis, with elements omitted from the first colon supplied from the second colon, is attested in biblical poetry. Verse 8b could then be translated, "not in vision and enigma," these two terms corresponding to the two expressions used in verse 6 to describe revelation given to the prophets. Verse 8 as a whole would then exhibit the following chiastic structure: positive (8a). negative (8b). positive (8c).

Lord as his special confidant, as his mouth in the revelation of his holy covenant with its righteous stipulations, as the one "whom the Lord knew face to face" (Deut. 34:10). And the formal-physical element of the glory-image had its classic Old Testament expression in the transfiguration of his countenance in reflection of the light of the theophanic Glory.

But our more specific concern at present is to trace the typological correspondence of Moses, mediator of the old covenant, to Jesus, mediator of the new covenant, in respect to his transmission to others of the divine likeness that was so conspicuously present in him. In this connection it may first be noted that both Moses and Jesus are presented as paradigms of the image they mediate to others. Christ is the exemplar for believers; they are predestined to be conformed to his image (Rom. 8:29). Investiture with Christ is synonymous with investiture with the image of God.[30] As the image of the first Adam is borne by all who trace descent to him, so we who are the sons of Jesus in the Spirit shall bear his glory-image.[31] Similarly, Moses was the paradigm for the prophets, and thus the paradigm of the prophetic *imago Dei*. Once again we recall that in the primary constitutional provision for the office of prophet it is said that the prophets will be like unto Moses (Deut. 18:15, 18). Though not the equal of Moses,[32] the Israelite prophet was a prophet after the order of Moses. As a bearer of the prophetic *imago Dei,* he bore the image of Moses, the paradigm prophet.

Beyond his serving as a paradigm for the prophets, Moses was instrumental in the actual impartation of his prophetic likeness to others—a further point in the typological correspondence to the mediatorial role of Jesus.

One instance of Moses' transmission of the prophetic image was his commissioning of Joshua to be his immediate successor. Though Joshua, like subsequent Israelite prophets, was not the equal of Moses, he was indeed a prophet-ruler like unto Moses, in fact, peculiarly so. As a privilege attendant on his position as minister to Moses, Joshua

---

30. See p. 35.
31. Cf. I Corinthians 15:48, 49.
32. Cf. Numbers 12:6–8; (Heb. 3:3–5); Deuteronomy 34:10–12.

stood in the Glory-council.[33] Significantly, his commissioning to prophetic office took place in the presence of the Lord revealed in the
Glory-pillar at the door of the tabernacle (Deut. 31:14, 15).
Functionally, Joshua was the prophet-mediator of God's covenant rule:
he mediated the divine word of direction and discipline to Israel[34] and
officiated in covenant ratification and renewal.[35] Joshua's duplication
of the Mosaic sign of the miraculous crossing of the waters emphati-
cally attested that the Lord was exalting him to be the successor-
likeness of Moses.[36]

Moses commissioned Joshua by the ritual of the laying on of
hands.[37] Deuteronomy 34:9 attributes to this act of ordination by
Moses the fact that Joshua was full of the Spirit-endowment of wisdom. What transpired in this communication of the Spirit through
Moses is described in Numbers 27:20 as a bestowal of Moses' own
majesty or splendor, (hôḏ) on Joshua. This hôḏ is royal glory,[38] or even
more concretely, the robe of glory with which the king was invested.[39]
According to this conceptualization, to commission to prophetic office
after the order of Moses was to invest with that royal glory that is of the
essence of the *imago Dei*.

Numbers 11 records an event in which Moses played a similar
mediatorial role. At least, this episode involves a distribution to others
of the Spirit with which Moses was richly endued. Though the re-
cipients were not called to the prophetic office they did engage in
"prophesying" through their participation in the Spirit of Moses. They
also shared, as we shall see, in Moses' judicial glory, that central
element of the *imago Dei*.

A preliminary comment is necessary about the arrangement of the
Pentateuchal narrative. Numbers 11:10ff. and Exodus 18 belong together. Chronologically, the Exodus 18 episode comes at the end of

---

33. Cf., e.g., Exodus 24:13ff.; 33:11.
34. Cf., e.g., Joshua 3:9ff.; 6:2ff.; 7:10ff.; 23:2ff.
35. Cf. Joshua 8:30ff.; 24:1ff.
36. Cf. Joshua 3:7; 4:14.
37. Cf. Numbers 27:18, 23.
38. Cf., e.g., I Chronicles 29:25; Psalms 45:3(4); 145:5.
39. Cf., e.g., Job 40:10; Psalm 104:1; Zechariah 6:13. The imagery of the Moses-
Joshua succession as described in Numbers 27:20 would then be comparable to the
symbolism of the mantle in the Elijah-Elisha succession (II Kings 2:13, 14).

Israel's stay at Sinai, the literary location of the chapter being dictated by considerations of literary themes and structures. A full investigation of this turns up some interesting exegetical points but would lead us too far astray. It must suffice to call attention to the overlapping of the subject matter of Exodus 18 and Numbers 10:29–32 and especially to the fact that the historical review of the Sinai encampment in Deuteronomy 1 locates the Exodus 18 episode at the later time dealt with from Numbers 10 on. Indeed, the Exodus 18 provision for judicial assistants for Moses is introduced in Deuteronomy 1:9ff. by reference to the complaint of Moses recorded in Numbers 11:11ff. It is because this relationship of Numbers 11 to Exodus 18 is assumed in Numbers 11 that the narrative there does not specify what function the seventy elders were to perform in order to lighten Moses' burden. It is understood that they are the men mentioned in Exodus 18 as appointed to assist Moses in his judicial tasks.

Investing of the seventy elders with judicial authority was again a matter of transmitting to others the Spirit possessed in abundance by Moses. Qualification for judicial office was found in the Spirit and his gift of governmental wisdom. The "prophesying" done by the seventy was a temporary phenomenon (Num. 11:25). This gift of the Spirit was not equipment for the performance of official functions but an introductory certification of divine appointment.

The terminology of the account of the distribution of the Spirit of Moses to the seventy in Numbers 11:17 and 25, the verb 'āṣal in particular, suggests perhaps that Moses is thought of as a father transmitting the inheritance to his sons. For 'āṣal, "withdraw, reserve," is the word used by Esau when he asks whether Isaac has not reserved a blessing for him, even though the firstborn's blessing has been granted to Jacob (Gen. 27:36). Might then the situation in Numbers 11 be that Joshua[40] was viewed as Moses' "firstborn"[41] but a share in the Spirit of Moses was reserved for the seventy? Or does 'āṣal simply convey the idea of withdrawing the Spirit from Moses regarded as repository of the Spirit—a withdrawal without diminution, as with the widow's

---

40. Cf. Numbers 11:28, 29.
41. Compare Elisha's reception of the firstborn's double share of the Spirit of his "father" Elijah (II Kings 2:9–12).

cruse of oil? Either way, what was transmitted in this case would be Moses' own nature, as it were, as bearer of the Spirit.[42] The transmission of the Spirit to the seventy elders was then akin to an act of fathering, as when Adam, bearer of God's image, begat Seth in his own image.[43] However the verb 'āṣal is construed, the impartation of the Spirit to the seventy, creative act of God himself though it ultimately was, is depicted in Numbers 11 as a transmission of that which Moses had to others. Moses was mediator of the Spirit who rested upon him and he thereby functioned mediatorially in the reproduction of the glory-image in the seventy.

Relevant also, along with the instances of Moses mediating the Spirit to Joshua and the seventy, are his acts of anointing with the holy oil, symbol of the Spirit. In the Old Testament Pentecost event of Exodus 40, Moses symbolically mediated the Spirit to the tabernacle and to the Aaronic priesthood by such anointing,[44] so anticipating in symbolic ritual the descent of the Glory-cloud itself to fill the tabernacle with glory.[45] In the light of the symbolic significance of the tabernacle and Aaron's vestments as images of the Glory-Spirit, the work of Moses—his supervisory role in the entire process of the construction and erection of the tabernacle and in the making and putting on of the priests' vestments, and his culminating act of anointing—becomes a notable adumbration of Christ's mediatorial re-creation of his temple-priest-people in the image of God.[46]

Our treatment of Moses' transmission of his prophetic image has developed into a discussion of his mediating of the Spirit. Naturally enough, for the prophetic image is a special form of the *imago Dei* and

---

42. The Elijah-Elisha parallel is again instructive, for the inheritance received was investiture with the mantle-likeness of Elijah, whereby he duplicated his "father's" glory-sign.
43. Cf. Genesis 5:1-3.
44. Cf. Exodus 28:41; 40:9-16.
45. Cf. Exodus 40:34. See. p. 46.
46. Relevant to Moses' mediation of the Spirit to Israel is Paul's interpretation of the exodus event as a "baptism into Moses" in the cloud and in the sea (I Cor. 10:2). This reflects the remarkable correlation of Moses with Yahweh in the Book of Exodus, where it is said that the result of the saving revelation of God's Presence was a realization of the purpose that Israel should both fear Yahweh and believe in Moses as the prophet-mediator of that saving Presence (14:30, 31; cf. 4:5; 19:9).

investment with the *imago Dei* is one with the filling of the Spirit. This merging of biblical concepts arises from the identity of the Spirit-Glory as the one who was the paradigm for the *imago Dei* and who creatively replicated the image.[47] Pentecost is then a New Testament creation of man in God's Spirit-likeness, a redemptive recapitulation of Genesis 1:2 and 27. In this New Testament event the Lord Christ endows his church with the Spirit and in so doing produces a likeness of the Spirit, an image of the Glory. In the Old Testament version of Pentecost, as we have found in tracing the Old Testament prophetic model of the image, Moses performed a prototypal messianic role as mediator of the Spirit and thereby of the (prophetic) *imago Dei*.

The Angel of the Presence

The Angel and Deity

Within the history of prophetic administration of God's covenant with Israel a second figure appears who acts as a mediator of the Glory-Spirit and transmitter of the prophetic image. Moses was the paradigm prophet, but this second figure was the original paradigm prophet behind the paradigm prophet Moses. He was a divine paradigm—not the Glory-Presence as such but the one whom Isaiah called "the Angel of the Presence" (Isa. 63:9), the one the church has recognized as Christ the Lord in preincarnation manifestation.[48]

The personal identification of the Angel of the Lord with Christ follows from various biblical data. The Angel's possession of the divine nature is expressly affirmed in God's declaration that his "name" was "in" the Angel (Exod. 23:21). In the biblical contexts referring to the Angel from Genesis on[49] there is an oscillation between him and God and there is no satisfactory accounting for this alternation in all the variety of circumstances in the relevant passages apart from the recognition that the Angel was a form of God's self-manifestation. The place where the Angel appeared was by virtue of his presence holy ground, a divine sanctuary to be guarded against profanation, hence mandating

---

47. See p. 21f. Here again we may mention the correlation of the biblical concepts of the *imago Dei* and messiahship, with its Spirit charism and commissioning.
48. See p. 17.
49. In Genesis see 16:7–14; 21:17; 22:11–16; 31:11–13; 48:15, 16.

the removal of profaned shoes.[50] His was the exclusively divine prerogative to forgive sin.[51] Malachi, calling him "the Angel of the covenant," equates his coming with the coming of the Lord (Mal. 3:1).

We are particularly interested here in the interrelationship of the Angel of the Lord and the Glory-Spirit. The oscillation we have mentioned in the texts is at times specifically between the Angel and God's theophanic revelation in the Glory-cloud. Thus, in Exodus 14:19 the statement that the Angel of God moved from before to the rear of the Israelite hosts is paralleled by the statement that the pillar of cloud did so. For reflections on the exodus event making the same identification, see Numbers 20:16 and Isaiah 63:9.[52]

Although the Angel is identified with God, he may also be distinguished as one who is sent by God on a mission or who himself refers to the Lord in the third person. In this fact that the Angel is distinguishable from God, there is a basis for his being a prophet-figure, even though also a divine figure.

More particularly, Angel of the Presence though he is, this Angel may be distinguished from the Glory-Presence theophany. The subtleties of this mysterious relationship have perplexed the exegesis of Exodus 32 and 33. Some commentators feel that the difficulties encountered in these chapters compel the assumption that the present narrative combines sources which were not in agreement on their theology of the divine presence in Israel. It will be found, I believe, that a satisfactory solution depends on our recognizing that the negotiations of the Lord and Moses turn on the distinction between the Angel and the Presence.

In response to the intercession of Moses on this occasion of his second forty days on the mount, the Lord promised to send the Angel ("my Angel," Exod. 32:34) before Israel to drive out the occupants of the promised land with a view to Israel's possessing it (Exod. 32:34 and 33:1, 2). In contrast to the promise of the availability of the Angel was the Lord's declaration: "I will not go up in your midst" (Exod.

---

50. Cf. Exodus 3:5; Joshua 5:15.
51. Cf. Exodus 23:21.
52. Cf. also Exodus 3:2ff.

33:3). Relenting, however, at Moses' further plea that God's royal splendor or Majesty[53] should go with them (Exod. 33:12, 13),[54] the Lord promised: "My Presence will go" (Exod. 33:14). This prompted Moses to express the desire to proceed no farther unless the Lord's Presence did indeed accompany him and the people (Exod. 33:15), for it was in God's going with them that his election of Israel would be known (Exod. 33:16). Moreover, as a seal of God's assurance that he would do this (Exod. 33:17), Moses requested a revelation of God's Glory (Exod. 33:18). Associated with the Presence-Face in distinction from the Angel in this narrative are the Glory (*derek*, v. 13, and *kābôd*, v. 18) and God's own going in the midst of Israel.

The issue concerned two modes of divine manifestation—one that had been characteristic of the patriarchal age and one that signalized the new Mosaic age of the fulfillment of the promises. During the earlier period when the kingdom offered in the Abrahamic promises was still abeyant, God appeared as the Angel, apart from the Glory phenomena. But the advent of the age that was prototypal of final judgment and kingdom consummation witnessed a form of theophany appropriate to an age of eschatological fulfillment. God's self-revelation to Israel in this age of exodus triumph and kingdom founding was

---

53. The exegesis of Exodus 33:13, with its textual uncertainties, is difficult. The interpretation of Moses' request presented above involves the recognition that this verse contains another instance of the word *derek* in the sense "dominion, power, throne" (cf. Ugaritic *drkt*). I would translate it here "(royal) Splendor" or "Majesty," signifying a visible entity, and add it to the list of designations for the Glory theophany. Some other possible examples of this usage may be suggested. They are from challenging poetic passages and only a bare indication can be given here of how I would interpret them. Psalm 77:13(14) may be translated: "O God, your Majesty surpasses that of the holy ones; what god is greater than you, O God?" The supremacy of God is then illustrated in verses 14–16(15–17) by his triumph over the "sea" at the exodus, when the sight of the theophanic "Arm" struck panic into "the great waters." Verse 19a(20a), harking back to the form of verse 13a (with its comparative use of the preposition *b*-) concludes: "Your Majesty surpassed that of the sea." If M. Dahood is correct (*Psalms, II, The Anchor Bible* [New York: Doubleday, 1968], p. 233), verse 19b(20b) refers to the train of the theophanic Glory (the imagery of Isa. 6:1). In that case, we would translate: "Your Majesty was upon the sea, and the train of your Glory was upon the great waters" (vv. 19a and b). In Psalm 138:5, *derek* is paralleled by *kābôd*: "They will sing of the Majesty of Yahweh: 'Great is the Glory of Yahweh.'" Note also the close association of *derek* with *pānîm*, "Glory-Presence," in Psalm 67:1, 2(2, 3).
54. Exodus 33:4–11 is a dischronologized parenthesis. See further on this below.

still a revelation through the Angel, but now the Angel appeared in union with the Spirit-Presence, in the more public and continuous and awesome epiphany of the Glory-cloud. This Old Testament pattern of theophany has its antitypical parallel in the successive states of humiliation and exaltation in the history of the incarnate Son, whose triumphant exodus entrance into the heavenly kingdom is marked by his investiture in the clouds of glory as the glorified Spirit-Lord.

The basic issue then in the Exodus 32 and 33 negotiations was whether the Glory-Presence of God, the Shekinah cloud clearly visible to all far and wide, would continue with Israel or whether there would be a return to the more private mode of theophany in the form of intermittent appearances of the Angel apart from the Glory. What Moses desired was the clearest possible assurance of the restoration of the covenantal favor of God that had been forfeited in Israel's breaking of the covenant in the matter of the golden calf. His concern was to secure certification of his own mediatorial vocation before the eyes of Israel and attestation of Israel's election as God's kingdom people before the eyes of the Egyptians and other nations.[55] Only a manifestation of God's presence with the awesome public visibility of the Glory-cloud could accomplish these ends. Since the fame of the spectacular divine presence in Israel's midst had already spread among the surrounding nations, it would be particularly difficult to convince them of Israel's status as God's protectorate if the famous Glory theophany were now withdrawn.

The point of Moses' intercession in Exodus 32 and 33 hinges on the distinction between Angel-theophany and Presence-Face-theophany, or better, between Glory-Angel theophany and Angel theophany apart from the Glory-Face. But another related matter in this passage requires clarification, namely, the distinction between God's Glory-Presence in the center of Israel's camp and its location outside the camp. This theme enters the narrative in connection with the reason God gave for withdrawing his Glory-Presence and reverting to Angel theophany: God warned that the Glory-Presence would threaten the very existence of a people like Israel. If the presence of the Glory

---

55. Cf. Exodus 32:11-14 (which belongs to the intercession of the second forty days) and 33:12-15.

signified the arrival of an age of eschatological fulfillment of covenant blessings, it meant by the same token undelayed execution of covenant curses. If it meant prompt, devastating judgment on the Egyptians and other enemies of Israel, it meant also that God would in a moment consume Israel too, if they rebelled—and they had already demonstrated their proclivity for that (Exod. 33:3, 5). Having been introduced into the narrative in this way, the theme of the location of the Glory among the Israelites was then pursued in Exodus 33:4-11 beyond the immediate historical situation in view in the context, before the narrative of the second forty days of Moses on Sinai continued again at Exodus 33:12. In the dischronologized section, Exodus 33:4-11, it is related how the problem envisaged by the Lord materialized and was dealt with after the departure from Horeb about a year later. By that time, although God granted Moses' plea for the accompanying presence of the Glory-cloud, Israel had rebelled again and had come under the sentence of a generation of wandering short of Canaan. Nevertheless, the Lord, faithful to his commitment that his Presence would continue with Israel (Exod. 33:14), did not remove the Shekinah entirely. He did, however, reposition the Glory-Spirit outside the camp, putting a distance between the Spirit of judgment and the rebellious people, lest Israel should not survive to enter the kingdom land eventually. Exodus 33:7-11 describes this development in terms of a relocating of the Glory-Spirit's dwelling place, the tabernacle (which had been built by then, as is related in Exodus 25-40).[56] These verses also indicate how the tabernacle's new location outside the camp affected the circumstances of God's revelation of himself through the Glory-pillar to Israel's mediator.

The question of the particular location of the Glory and the tabernacle, whether in the center or outside the camp of Israel, was not the subject of Moses' intercession during his second forty days on Sinai. His concern then was rather with the different modes of Angel-theophany, whether with or without the Glory-Spirit. According to Exodus 32 and 33, though there is a metaphysical bonding of the Angel

---

56. Mention of the tent of meeting, or assembly, in Exodus 33:7ff. is one of several indications that this passage develops its theme beyond the chronological setting of the surrounding literary context.

and the Glory-Spirit, the Angel is distinguishable and separable from the Glory. And now we can refine our earlier observation: the basis for the prophet-identity of the Angel is found in this relationship of the Angel to the Glory-Spirit as one who belonging to the Glory was also sent forth to the covenant people.

The Angel as a Prophet

As one who was integral to the Glory from the beginning, the Angel of the Presence enjoyed as an original prerogative that standing in the heavenly council which was prerequisite to true prophethood. And as the divine *mal'āk*, "messenger, angel," sent forth from that Glory-council,[57] he was the original of all the prophet-"messengers" (*mal'ākîm*). Like the prophets raised up after the order of Moses, the Angel had a covenantal mission—Malachi calls him "the Angel of the covenant" (Mal. 3:1) and Yahweh, speaking as Lord of the covenant in "the book of the covenant," calls him "my Angel" (Exod. 23:23). The directive given Israel in the Deuteronomic law of the prophet to heed the words of the prophets under threat of the covenant curses for failure to do so (Deut. 18:15, 19) was an extension of the orders God gave earlier respecting his Angel, this too in the context of the covenant sanctions: "Obey his voice and provoke him not" (Exod. 23:21a). The authority of the prophets was the delegated divine authority of those who spoke in the name of God (Deut. 18:19); divine authority was original with the Angel-prophet for God's name was "in him" (Exod. 23:21c). But perhaps the Angel's identity as a prophet figure—as the divine paradigm prophet of whom the other prophets were human images—comes into its sharpest focus in a series of passages in the Book of Judges where he is depicted as messenger of the covenant engaged in that prophetic function so prominent in the Old Testament, the prosecution of Yahweh's covenant lawsuit against Israel.[58]

Judges 2:1-3 recounts a coming of the Angel of the Lord in the course of the occupation of the land to confront the Israelites with their failure to obey the Lord's demand for the total destruction of the

---

57. Cf. Exodus 23:20ff.; 33:2; Zechariah 2:9, 11(13, 15).
58. Cf., e.g., II Kings 17:13–18; II Chronicles 36:15, 16.

Canaanites. In its form the Angel's message follows the general pattern of covenant lawsuit speeches as attested elsewhere in the Bible, particularly in the prophetical books. a.) A reminder of Yahweh's claims on Israel's allegiance, expressed in an historical review of his leadership hitherto (v. 1). In fulfillment of his promissory oath to the patriarchs he had brought them out of Egypt into Canaan and had committed himself to continuing faithfulness as their covenant Lord. b.) The indictment of Israel (v. 2). This consists of a reminder that the Lord had stipulated in his covenant that Israel was not to entangle themselves in alliances with the idolatrous Canaanites and a rebuke for their disobedience (couched in the interrogative style characteristic of this element in the lawsuit). c.) The threat of judgment (v. 3). The Lord will not completely eliminate the Canaanites from before the advancing Israelites.

In the Song of Deborah there is a reference to the Angel performing a similar function (Judg. 5:23). The prophetess reports that the Angel of the Lord had pronounced a curse against those who had refused to comply with the covenantal demand to supply troops for the holy war of the Lord.

Then in Judges 6:8–10 we read of a prophet (*nābî'*) sent to Israel with a lawsuit message that is very much like that of the Angel of the Lord in Judges 2:1–3. It asserts the Lord's claim on Israel's loyal service by quoting his self-identification from the treaty preamble: "I am the Lord your God" (v. 10a) and by recalling his action on Israel's behalf in the exodus and conquest (vv. 8, 9). By way of indictment, Israel is reminded of the command not to submit to the gods of the Amorites (v. 10b) and denounced for their violations (v. 10c). The implicit sentence, reconstructed from the introductory explanation of the occasion of the prophet's mission (v. 7), is that the Lord will continue to afflict Israel by the hand of the Midianites if they persist in their idolatrous disobedience. To suggest that the person called "a prophet" in verse 8 is the Angel of the Lord may seem too bold, yet that identification is possibly correct. Neither the statement that the Lord sent the prophet nor the prophet's own use of the messenger formula, "Thus says the Lord," disallows this interpretation.[59] More-

---

59. For the Angel's use of the messenger formula, see Zechariah 3:6, 7; cf. Genesis 22:16.

over, in the immediately following verse (Judg. 6:11), as the narrative of God's response to Israel's cry continues, there is an explicit reference to the Angel of the Lord, now on mission to Gideon to summon him to deliver Israel from the Midianites. On this interpretation, we would then have in Judges 6:8 a remarkably direct identification of the Angel of the Lord as a "prophet."[60] But even if the prophet of this episode is not the Angel of the Lord, the very close correspondence between the missions and messages of the Angel in Judges 2:1-3 and the figure called "prophet" in Judges 6:8-10 would still serve the purpose of clearly identifying the Angel as one who performed the prophetic office.

We come upon another covenant lawsuit episode in Judges 10:11-14. This time the text states, "And the Lord said to the Israelites" (v. 11). Since, in passages where the Angel appears, references to him as simply "the Lord" alternate with the full designation "the Angel of the Lord,"[61] we are probably to understand that it was the Angel of the Lord who conveyed the lawsuit message of Judges 10:11-14. In form and substance this speech is essentially the same as the others we have analyzed. It consists of Yahweh's claims (vv. 11, 12—the historical resumé of divine deliverances being brought up to date, as was done in the historical prologues of the ancient treaties when they were renewed); the indictment, specifying apostasy (v. 13a); and the sentence threatening abandonment (v. 13b). In addition, there is another feature common in lawsuit addresses, namely, a warning of the futility of appealing to other helpers (v. 14).

Judges 13:3ff. does not describe a lawsuit episode but it should be included in our list of passages from the Book of Judges because it

---

60. A case might be made for finding a similar instance in Hosea 12:13(14), particularly if we translate $b^e n\bar{a}\underline{b}\hat{i}$' "by a prophet." There is a reference to the Angel in the context; see verse 4(5). But in view of the parallelism of the terms used in verses 12 and 13 (13 and 14), it is probably better to translate "for the sake of a prophet" to match "for the sake of a wife" in verse 12(13). Thus understood, the reference might be to the intercessory role of Moses by which Israel was spared more than once. This would suit well the contextual emphasis on waiting on God for his mercy and help; see verses 4-6(5-7). A further possibility is that the reference is to the prophet-intercessor, Abraham (cf. Gen. 20:7; Ps. 105:15), or Jacob (cf. Hos. 12:4, 5[5, 6]), since the Lord's deliverance and preservation of Israel was in remembrance of covenant promises made to Abraham, Isaac, and Jacob (see, e.g., Ps. 105:8ff., 42; cf. Mic. 7:20).
61. Cf., e.g., Zechariah 1:12, 13; 3:1, 2.

contains a most circumstantial account of a remarkable appearance of the Angel, in which he performs the basic messenger function of the prophets.[62] While the Angel is clearly distinguishable from God in this episode, his divine identity is also strongly attested here (see especially vv. 18–23). He comes foretelling the birth to a barren woman of one by whom God will deliver his people. This prophetic word is in the tradition of birth announcements made by the Angel back in the patriarchal period,[63] a tradition that was continued later in the prophetic movement as Isaiah announced the advent of Immanuel by virgin birth to bring peace to his people (Isa. 7:14ff.). So prophet-like an impression is conveyed by the Angel that Manoah and his wife, not yet knowing he was the Angel of the Lord (v. 16), refer to him as "the man of God" (vv. 6, 8), a designation synonymous with $nābî'$, "prophet."[64] In keeping with that understanding of the Angel, Manoah applies to his message the terms of the Deuteronomic test of a true prophet (vv. 12, 17; cf. Deut. 18:22).

From this series of passages in Judges it is evident that when Yahweh was first instituting the process of covenant lawsuit administration after Israel's entry into Canaan under Joshua, he did so through the agency of his Angel. Subsequently, the succession of prophets would continue the prosecution of this divine lawsuit down through the centuries to the tragedy of the exile and dispersion in which it eventually issued. In doing so, they followed the pattern set for them by the Angel of the Lord, the divine paradigm prophet.

A more complete comparison of the activities of the Angel and the Israelite prophets, drawing upon the evidence of the pre-Mosaic and other appearances of the Angel, would show that he was the archetype of the prophets in the broader aspects of their vocation too, including the role of priestly intercession and the royal task of building and destroying nations. But for now we may rest the case for the identification of the Angel of the Lord as paradigm of the prophets with the

---

62. As an additional explicit reference to the Angel on prophetic mission during the period of the judges, this episode strengthens the plausibility of identifying the lawsuit prosecutor in Judges 6:8-10 and 10:11-14 as the Angel.

63. Cf. Genesis 16:11, 12; 18:10ff.

64. The "man of God" designation is used for Moses and Samuel, for Elijah and Elisha, and for other named and anonymous prophets. In Akkadian texts the expression "man of X" is used instead of the term "messenger" for individuals with more authority than simple couriers.

observation that revelation by the Angel mode was phased out syn-chronously with the phasing in of the prophetic movement.[65] Clearly, the prophets took up the task that the Angel had previously performed. And because of this manifest continuity of the prophets with the Angel of the Lord, the foundational mission of the Angel, with the Glory theophany and miracle signs that accompanied it, served from the outset as a mighty certification of the divine origin of the word of the prophets, the successors of this Angel-prophet.

The Angel as Mediator of the Image

Archetype prophet that he was, the Angel of the Lord reproduced his prophet-likeness in human ectypes. As the Creator-Spirit of Genesis 1:2 replicated his Glory-image in man at the beginning, so by creative action the Angel embodiment and mediatorial agent of the Glory-Spirit replicated in Moses and the prophets the prophetic *imago Dei* of which he was himself the divine paradigm.

This process of reproduction of the prophetic Glory-image is most plainly observable in the experience of the human paradigm prophet, particularly in the illumination of Moses' countenance. The disclosure of the divine Glory immediately associated with Moses' initial trans-figuration experience was one that involved not simply the descent of the Glory-cloud but the appearance of a glorious figure whom Moses might see only from the back. This figure is to be identified as the Angel of the Presence.[66] Previously the Angel had appeared to men apart from the Glory-cloud, with his heavenly glory temporarily laid

---

65. In "Angel-Prophet or Satan-Prophet?", *Zeitschrift für die alttestamentliche Wis-senschaft* 82 (1970): 31–67, Robert North works out a sequence of six stages of "divine communications-media." I find the scheme as such unacceptable, for one thing, because of the distortion it suffers from higher critical misdating of the sources. But relevant to our discussion above is North's identification of two successive "mes-senger" stages: the first divine communication through the *mal'āk* (God himself being meant in the early occurrences); and the second, through the *nābî'* (pp. 33f., 38). While recognizing, in effect, the prophet's messenger function in the role of the divine *mal'āk*, North does not notice that that role also involves the *rîb*, "lawsuit," function of the prophets (in North's terminology, the Satan-prophet function). Edmond Jacob, observing that the Angel of Yahweh is not mentioned by the major prophets, wonders whether the place held by the Angel was not assumed by the prophets. See his *Theology of the Old Testament* (New York: Harper, 1958), p. 77.

66. At Moses' original call it was the Angel of the Lord who appeared to him in the fiery theophany of the burning bush (Exod. 3:2).

aside, but now, as a seal of God's promise to lead Israel into Canaan not by the Angel apart from the Presence but together with the Glory-Presence, he was revealed to Moses in his Glory-form. And by the creative power of this visible confrontation with Moses in the Glory theophany, the Angel-prophet transmitted to Moses the likeness of his own prophetic glory.[67]

Such an understanding of that event on the part of the people of Israel themselves seems to be reflected in the Judges 13 episode of the Angel's appearance to the mother-to-be of Samson. In reporting the occurrence to her husband, she described the "man of God" who came to her as of fearful appearance like the Angel of God (v. 6). We can most readily explain her thought process if we assume she was familiar with the Exodus 34 story of the shining countenance of the original "man of God" and with a traditional interpretation of the awesome theophany seen by Moses on that occasion in terms of the Angel of the Lord.[68]

The intermediary role of the Angel in the formation of the prophets who were raised up after the order of Moses is suggested by those passages which, rather than tracing directly to the Spirit the communication of God's revelation to the prophets, attribute this to the Angel.[69] This role of the Angel is most prominent in the biblical record in connection with the Horeb experience of the man of God, Elijah, which so remarkably recapitulated the Exodus 34 theophany-transfiguration experience of Moses.

From what is expressly stated of the Angel's intermediary functioning in the history of the foundational prophetic figures, Moses and Elijah, the two whose lives most dramatically exhibit the re-creation and glorification of the *imago Dei*, we may gather that he had a similar part in the rapture of the other prophets into the Spirit-council, where they were endowed with the Spirit and made partakers of the likeness of the Glory.

Of special interest for the theme of the Angel of the Lord as creator of the divine image in men is the visionary episode of Zechariah 3. In

---

67. Cf. Exodus 33:13ff.; 34:5ff., 29ff.
68. For another link between the two contexts, this one also involving the theme of the fearful nature of divine epiphany, see Exodus 33:20 and Judges 13:22.
69. See, e.g., I Kings 19:5, 7; II Kings 1:3, 15; I Chronicles 21:18; cf. I Kings 13:18.

this vision the Angel sovereignly supervises the process of clothing the highpriest of Israel with the holy garments of his office, the investiture process that we have found to be symbolic of the re-creation of the people of God in the image of the Glory-Spirit. The Old Testament thus assigns to the Angel of the Lord a mediatorial role in the re-creation of image-bearers of the Glory-Spirit when it is presenting that redemptive truth under the imagery of both the parallel models of priestly investiture and prophetic charism.[70]

Christ and the Prophetic Image

In this final major section of this chapter we shall observe how the prophetic model of the *imago Dei* is appropriated by biblical, especially New Testament, writers for their delineation of re-creation in the image of God in Christ Jesus. To do so we must first review the identity of Jesus as the antitypical Moses-prophet and as the incarnation of the Angel of the Lord.

Jesus as Antitypical Moses-Prophet

Deuteronomy 18:15–22, defining "prophet" in terms of Moses as paradigm, provides the constitutional basis for the Old Testament covenantal office of the prophet. But because of the typological nature of Israel's theocratic officers, they point beyond themselves to their messianic antitype; hence, the constitutional provision of Deuteronomy 18 for the succession of Old Testament prophets is also a promise of the ultimate individual prophet of the new covenant. Agreeably, Peter affirmed that Jesus was this prophet like unto Moses (Acts 3:22f.).[71] The apostle had grasped the significance of the event of Jesus' transfiguration, recognizing it as a counterpart to Moses' experience under the overshadowing Glory-cloud at Sinai. In the command of the voice from heaven, "Hear him," Peter perceived the

---

70. A fusion of the two models is found in Elijah's conveying of his Spirit-likeness to Elisha by investing him with his mantle. See footnotes 41 and 42 for the motif of transmission of the *imago Dei* from father to son in the Elijah-Elisha succession. Note too in the same historical context the prominence of the "sons of the prophets" in association with Elijah and Elisha.
71. Cf. John 5:43; 12:48ff.; Matthew 17:5.

ultimate application of the Deuteronomic requirement that Israel obey God's prophet (Deut. 18:18). That was God's own identification of Jesus as *the* prophet like unto Moses. The pattern set by Moses was fully matched (and, of course, more than matched) in Jesus. For, like Moses, Jesus is prophet-mediator of the covenant not only in the sense of performing the function of authoritative spokesman in the ongoing covenantal administration, but he was also mediator of the covenant in its inauguration.[72]

An intermediate connection in biblical revelation between Moses and Jesus, the fulfillment of the prophet-paradigm, is the Isaianic Servant of the Lord. For, on the one hand, in speaking of the Servant, the prophet spoke of Christ, and, on the other, Isaiah portrays that Servant as a new Moses-prophet. The servant is raised up by the elective call of God (42:1, 6; 49:1) and Spirit-endowed (42:1; 61:1); he is cognizant of the divine counsel (50:4f.) and made an effective "mouth" for the Lord (49:2; 50:4; 61:1f.); and he is mediator of the redemptive covenant in fulfillment of covenantal promises of deliverance and kingdom inheritance through righteous judgment (42:1ff., 6ff.; 49:5ff.; 53:4ff.; 61:1ff.).

Jesus Christ is the ultimate realization of the Moses-Servant-prophet. He is a participant in the Glory of the heavenly council of the sons of God, and indeed, from eternity, in the Glory of the communion within the Godhead; possessing the Spirit without measure, he is sent forth from the Glory-council on covenantal mission as himself the living prophetic Word of God; he manifests his glory as the only-begotten of the Father, the true light; transfigured and exalted to the Glory of the Father's throne in the Spirit, he is priest-king builder of the kingdom of God and righteous judge-destroyer of Satan's kingdom. All that constitutes the prophetic *imago Dei* and had prototypal expression in the paradigm servant-prophet, Moses, is present in antitypical fulness in Jesus Christ.

Jesus, the Angel of the Lord Incarnate

Though Jesus comes later in time as the antitypical realization of the prophet-paradigm provided by Moses and prescribed in Deuteronomy

---

72. In my *SBA*, pp. 183–95, I have dealt more fully with the way the New Testament Gospels portray Jesus and his mission as a new Moses and new exodus.

18, he was before Moses. He appeared in Old Testament redemptive history in the theophanic form of the Angel. Jesus was that archetypal prophet behind the human prophet paradigm. He was the divine Angel-prophet who reproduced his prophet-likeness in Moses and the Moses-like prophets of the old covenant.

Quite apart from more specific biblical indications of the identity of Jesus Christ with the Angel of the Lord, that would be an inevitable deduction from the correspondence in the roles of these two divine figures in their respective economies. But the most obvious and direct disclosure of the personal identification of the two with each other is provided by Malachi 3. There, the Lord, who would appear in the great day of the Lord and come as a refiner to his temple, is called "the Angel of the covenant" (3:1), and the latter is clearly the Angel of the Lord, the agent of the Glory-Spirit in the establishment of the Mosaic Covenant. Since then this coming Lord, whose way was to be prepared by a *mal'āk* figure further described as "Elijah the prophet" (4:5 [3:23]), is, of course, the Lord Christ,[73] the Angel and Christ are one.

Zechariah 3 came to our attention above because it pictures the Angel of the Lord conducting the ritual of priestly investiture which is symbolic of putting on the glory-image. We return to it here for the further light it sheds on the identification of the Messiah with the Angel of the Lord. In the first part of the vision the Angel makes judicial disposition of an accusation brought against Joshua, the highpriest. After rebuking the accuser, the Angel turns to Joshua and first performs an act signifying the removal of Joshua's iniquity (v. 4) and then oversees the priestly investiture, the climax of the latter being the crowning with the mitre with its precious "stone," the engraved golden plate of consecration (v. 5).[74] In an explanatory statement in verse 9, we find that these are precisely the two things the Lord of hosts says he is going to accomplish. But he prefaces this declaration of purpose with the promise that he is going to bring forth his Servant, the Branch—that is, the Messiah (v. 8). The effect of that is to indicate that it will be in and through the Messiah (v. 8) that God will remove the iniquity of the land in one day and provide the consecration

---

73. Cf. Matthew 11:14; Mark 9:12; Luke 1:17.
74. My interpretation of the stone (v. 9) and various other features of this vision (hopefully to appear in an already very long delayed publication) can only be assumed here.

crown-stone as the completion of his reclothing of his people in the holy garments of his Glory-likeness (v. 9). The work of salvation performed by the Angel of the Lord in the visionary symbolism is thus attributed in the Lord's own prophetic exposition (voiced through the Angel, vv. 6f.) to the messianic Servant-Branch.

Revelation 10 may be cited as just one further passage identifying Christ as the Old Testament Angel. The Glory-Angel figure introduced there in the role of covenant witness is one and the same as the heavenly figure described in Daniel 10:5ff. (who appears also in Daniel 8:16 and 12:6ff.). Now, Daniel 10:5ff., along with the Daniel 7:9ff. vision of the Son of Man and Ancient of Days, stands behind the depiction of Christ as the incarnate Glory in Revelation 1:10ff. From this set of relationships it appears that the Book of Revelation made use of the figure of the Old Testament Glory-Angel in the same idiomatic way that it used numerous Old Testament prototypes to set forth the incarnate Lord Jesus. And it is also evident from all of this that the theophanic Angel was indeed a pre-incarnation manifestation of Christ.

The Prophetic Model in Messianic Re-creation of the Image of God

It is now to be observed that in some biblical passages dealing with the replication of the image of Christ in his people it is our Lord's identity as the prophet who fulfills the paradigm established by the Angel and Moses that is specifically in view, so that the church created in his image is also found in these passages to display a prophetic character. Our survey is necessarily only selective.

In II Corinthians 3 and 4, Paul describes the Christian's transformation into the image of the glory of the Lord in the terms of Moses' transfiguration. In this Pauline version, the counterpart to the prophet Moses is now the Christian believer and Christ corresponds to the Old Testament Angel of the Presence. Moses was transfigured by his face to face encounter with the Glory-Angel and the believer's transformation takes place as he beholds the glory of God in the face of Jesus Christ. Recourse to the Moses-prophet model to set forth creation in the Glory-image was natural in a context concerned with the church's prophetic mission of witness to the new covenant, particularly through the witness of the apostles. According to II Corinthians 3 and 4, for

Christ to re-create the church in his divine likeness is to create a prophet-church.

When observing in the preceding chapters that the theme of Christ's creation of the church in his image is fundamental in the structure of the Book of Revelation, we focused on the imagery of priestly investiture in the presentation of this idea. We may now supplement those comments by pointing to the way in which the Apocalypse also draws its imagery from the prophetic model in its development of this theme.

In Revelation 1, the idea of the fashioning of the church in the likeness of her glorified Lord is conveyed by portraying both Lord and church as luminous figures. Jesus, wrapped in Glory, the light of his face intense as the sun, stands in the midst of seven golden lampstands symbolic of the church.[75] Christ is the original light; the church which he creates in his likeness is a reflective light. The imagery of light-bearing objects itself speaks at once of prophetic witness.[76] And the lampstand imagery, taken from the Old Testament cultic lamps in the varying arrangements found in the tabernacle and the temple, distinctly symbolizes the covenant community bearing and communicating the glory of God's majestic name and truth in the midst of the nations. Once again then, in Revelation 1, the Glory-image of Christ is a prophetic image and the church created in his likeness is a prophet-church.

The lampstand symbol had received visionary exposition in the Old Testament in Zechariah 4. That passage is in view in Revelation 1 and again, and more obviously, when the lampstand imagery is used for the church in Revelation 11. It will be useful to look somewhat further into Zechariah 4 and Revelation 11.

In the vision of Zechariah 4, the golden lampstand is flanked by two olive trees and is so coupled to them that it receives a natural (that is, a divinely sustained) flow of the oil that fuels the bright burning of its seven lamps. The message of the chapter is that the covenant people will be empowered by God's Spirit, symbolized by the oil, to accomplish its prophetic light-bearing witness in the world (v. 6). That wit-

---

75. Note also the symbol of the stars for the "angels" of the churches (1:16, 20).
76. In the context, Jesus is described as "the faithful witness" (1:5) and the apostle as one devoted to "the word of God and the testimony of Jesus" (1:9).

ness was performed in the contemporary Old Testament situation chiefly by maintaining the theocratic cultus in the Jerusalem temple (vv. 7-10). What is to be stressed here is that according to the symbolic picture, the Spirit-oil is not only the source of energy for the lampstand but its paradigm as well. The golden nature of the lampstand (v. 2) corresponds to the color of the oil, which in a vivid metaphor is specifically called "the gold" (v. 12). Perhaps significant too is the use of the noun *yiṣhār* for this oil (v. 14), instead of *šemen*, usually used for anointing oil. For *yiṣhār* is related to a verb meaning to shine, and the thought might then be that the shining of the lamps is a replication of the oil's own nature.[77] We remarked earlier[78] that the priest by his anointing during the investiture ritual was saturated with the golden symbol of the Spirit or impregnated with the likeness of the Spirit, so that the anointing as well as the enrobing in the Glory-Spirit garments was a symbol of creation in the image of the Glory-Spirit. Such is the idea presented afresh in Zechariah 4—the Spirit, by filling the lampstand-community, creates his likeness in it, in particular, his prophetic likeness as covenant witness.

There is a great deal that might be said about the lineage of the symbolism of the two olive trees overarching the lampstand. To trace this would show these trees to be synonymous with symbols of the Glory-Spirit present in the holy of holies of the tabernacle and in the temple. They would be found to be figuratively equivalent to the cherubim-throne of the Glory overarching the ark and to the entrance pillars of the temple.[79] It would become evident that the two olive trees were representational of the Glory-Spirit under the particular aspect of the two-pillar theophany standing as witness to the covenant. Thus the creative-paradigm character of the Spirit in this Zechariah 4 symbolism would become the more apparent as the prophetic-witness nature of the lampstand was seen to answer in replica to that which was archetypally present in the nature of the olive trees.

---

77. The first replica of the Glory-Spirit to appear in the Genesis 1 creation record is the light that shone in the darkness over the deep (1:2, 3). Also fashioned in the likeness of the Glory were the luminaries of the fourth day and they provide an exact creation parallel to the lampstand luminaries in the redemptive pattern. On this, see further the following chapter, pp. 108, 110f., and 128.

78. See p. 45.

79. See p. 40.

Another feature that reinforces the prophet-witness motif in Zechariah 4 is the identification of the end-branches of the olive trees (presumably with their olive clusters) as "the two sons of oil" (v. 14). The frequent interpretation of these two as the royal and priestly offices, represented at the time by Zerubbabel and Joshua, is beset by the problem that the olive boughs with which they are identified are part of the source of the Spirit-oil, not a part of the receptive apparatus. Hence, the phrase "sons of oil" ought not to be understood in the sense of "anointed," which involves reception, not bestowal. This phrase is rather to be compared with an expression like "son of fatness (*šemen*)" in Isaiah 5:1, applied there to a hill to describe it as fertile. Whatever the idiomatic rendering of the phrase in English is to be, it should get across the idea that these two figures have a mediatorial function in the transmission of the Spirit-oil to the lampstand-community. Now, kings and priests were themselves anointed, but while priests on occasion participated in the anointing of others,[80] anointing was not a function of kings. It would appear then that "the two sons of oil" are to be interpreted as prophet figures. It is not necessary to think of two particular prophets, like Haggai and Zechariah or Moses and Elijah. Possibly there is an allusion to the law of witnesses requiring a minimum of two in certain cases, but this numerical element in the symbolism of the two olive trees and their two end-boughs (and the two "sons of oil") finds its origin and therewith its primary explanation in the two-pillar theophany, the feet of the Glory-witness, of which the imagery of the trees as a whole was (as we intimated above) a symbolic reflex. The prophets, outstandingly the paradigm prophet Moses, were God's chief agents for anointing. They anointed kings, notably founders of dynasties, and at the inauguration of the Aaronic priesthood, Moses anointed the priests. Moreover, when we take account not simply of officiating as anointers but of all that "sons of oil" would suggest by way of identification with the Spirit and rich possession of the Spirit, it becomes even more evident that the prophets are the most, if not the only, suitable candidates for these "sons of oil." The prophet was known as the "man of the Spirit." Anointing to office was not a mere matter of symbolic oil in

---

80. Cf., e.g., II Kings 11:12; II Chronicles 23:11.

the case of the prophets, but of the reality of the Spirit. Spiritual charism might attend the symbolic anointing of a king but the Spirit reality was essential to the identity of the true prophet. Only the office of the prophet was such that its holder might be regarded as standing with the Lord over against the covenant community—in the way required by the position of the olive trees with their end-boughs, symbol of "the sons of oil," over against the lampstand. Only the prophets were caught up in the Spirit into the divine council to have a place there among those heavenly servants who "stand by the Lord of all the earth,"[81] as "the two sons of oil" are said to do (v. 14). If then "the two sons of oil" and thereby the olive trees are to be interpreted as prophet-witnesses, this symbolic portrayal of creation in the image of the Glory-Spirit in Zechariah 4 is as explicitly prophetic in the case of the divine paradigm (the olive trees-Spirit) as in the case of the human replica (the lampstand-covenant people).

While the kind of Spirit-experience the prophets had justifies their being identified with the symbol of the source of the Spirit in Zechariah 4, such a function can be predicated of them only in a sense. Even in the case of Moses' communication of the Spirit to others, his role remained that of a secondary instrument and it was the Lord God himself who was and alone could be the real source and bestower of his Spirit. "The two sons of oil" in Zechariah 4 may be identified with the Old Testament prophets only in the limited sense that they were prototypal of the Lord Christ, the archetypal-antitypical prophet, who in the fullest measure possessed the Spirit, who was one with the Spirit, who was in truth the mediatorial source of the Spirit for his lampstand-church. Thus, Zechariah 4 not only contains the idea of the prophetic image of the Spirit and its reproduction in the witnessing people of God, but it points to Christ as the one who re-creates his prophet-likeness in his prophet-church.

All of this will be further confirmed when we examine Revelation 11, the other passage that uses the lampstand imagery found in Revelation 1—and, like Revelation 1, draws upon the imagery of Zechariah 4. But first, a couple of parenthetical comments on the two visions of Zechariah that have come under discussion in these pages.

---

81. Cf. Zechariah 3:4; 6:5.

Zechariah 3 and 4 present the two central visions in the chiastically structured night visions of the prophet (Zech. 1:7–6:8). As these visions develop the theme of the ultimate messianic restoration of God's kingdom, they place at the center of that redemptive accomplishment the renewal of the divine image in the new man in Christ Jesus. Employing in turn the priestly (Zech. 3) and prophetic (Zech. 4) models of the image of God and the mode of its replication, both chapters portray Christ as creator of his people in his own likeness. We are thus led to recognize that redemptive restoration as depicted in Old Testament typology and actualized in New Testament messianic reality is restoration (and consummation) of the creation order, and particularly restoration of man to the glory of that God-likeness in and for which he was created at the beginning. And we are alerted to the pervasive centrality of this foundational theme of Genesis 1 throughout the rest of the Scriptures.

Our other "parenthetical" comment actually gets us into things at the heart of the matter in these studies of the image of God. A question that is already placed before us by the general use throughout the Bible of the two conceptual models of the *imago Dei*, the priestly and prophetic, confronts us more clamantly in the striking side by side appearances of these two models in the successive night visions of Zechariah 3 and 4. It is the question of how the two models conceptually harmonize with one another. An attempt to answer this involves us in some elemental analysis of man and his historical mission and here I can only state briefly the general direction of my own thinking.

At the creation, God's image in man came to functional expression through man's royal-priestly office. As priest standing before the face of God, man received the glory of God in God's self-revelation in his Glory-Spirit and he returned glory to God in adoration. And as royal priest (kingship being ancillary to priesthood), man exercised dominion over God's holy world in the name of God and to his glory. The prophetic office, according to the specific biblical conception, belongs to the postlapsarian, redemptive situation, when certain men are separated out to stand over against other men as mediators of divine revelation. As seen in the prophets of Israel, the prophetic office involves priestly functions (e.g., altar ministry, intercession) and royal functions (e.g., judicial government). Thus, along with the conventional cult and court, along with Aaronic priest and Davidic king, a suprapriestly and suprakingly office existed in the prophet. The prophet possessed this royal-priesthood within a total commissioning that included his distinctive function as mediator of the covenant word from the heavenly council to Israel. But it was in those elements of the prophetic office that paralleled the institutional offices of priest and king that the prophetic likeness to the Glory-Spirit consisted. Hence, the office of the priest of the central sanctuary and the office of the priestly prophet both comprehended the priestly substance of the image of God, and accordingly the priestly and prophetic models of the image of God are entirely harmonious. The prophet and the highpriest were the two figures privileged to experience that personal confrontation with the Glory-Spirit that is creative of the divine likeness. This parallel between the two also brings out a difference. The highpriest beheld the Glory on the occasion of his annual entry into the earthly council-court. The prophet's Glory experience was his characteristic rapture into the heavenly council. The incorporation into the divine council in which man's divine likeness comes to eschatological perfection was then only symbolically portrayed in the priestly model of the *imago Dei;* but in the prophetic model, that eschatological destiny of redeemed mankind was proleptically anticipated in pneumatic reality.

Revelation 11 introduces the lampstand symbol anew, now as part of what is manifestly an adaptation of the Zechariah 4 imagery. In this adaptation (v. 4), the idea of a divine likeness replicated in a human image is highlighted. The correspondence between the divine original and the human replica in Zechariah 4 did not extend to the numerical aspect of the symbolism. But the Old Testament picture is altered in Revelation 11:4 so as to achieve numerical correspondence; there are now two lampstands to match the two olive trees. Furthermore, replication of the divine original in human images is a conspicuous motif in the overall portrayal of the two witnesses to whom the verse 4 symbolism refers. As their career unfolds in verses 3–12, the reader cannot miss the similarity of its pattern to that of Jesus' ministry. A time of proclamation and signs, issuing in Satanic opposition and the violent death of the witnesses in the great city, "where also our Lord was crucified" (so verse 8 adds, making the parallelism explicit), is followed by the resurrection of the martyrs and their ascension in a cloud.

It is, of course, the prophetic model that Revelation 11 employs in its treatment of divine image replication. The figures in whom the likeness of Christ is reproduced are expressly denoted as witnesses (v. 3) and prophets (vv. 10, 18) and their mission is described as one of prophesying (v. 3), prophecy (v. 6), and testimony (v. 7).[82] Moreover, the details of the picture of their mission come from the lives of Old Testament prophets, particularly Moses and Elijah. The three and a half years length of their witness (v. 3a) during which they restrain the rain (v. 6a) matches a period in Elijah's ministry of the same duration and character.[83] Threats against them are met by fiery destruction, as were those against Elijah.[84] And, like Moses, they execute plagues (v. 6b). There is also, of course, the identification of the two figures by the lampstand-witness imagery of Zechariah 4 (v. 4).[85]

In Revelation 11, it is the Lord Jesus who commissions the church as a prophet church in his own likeness. To see the whole picture properly it is necessary to look back into the tenth chapter. In Revelation 10, John is directed in his task as apocalyptic seer by the Glory-Angel, much as he was in Revelation 1 by Jesus, the incarnate Glory. A different Old Testament messianic figure is utilized in the two chapters, the Son of Man in chapter one and the Angel in chapter ten (both wrapped in the Glory-clouds), but it is the one and same Lord of John who commissions him in each episode.

According to Revelation 10:11, John is to prophesy before many

---

82. The usage of the expression "the testimony of Jesus" in the Book of Revelation brings out the prophetic nature of the Christian's witness and in particular its likeness to Jesus' own prophetic witness. In 1:2 it denotes the testimony given by Jesus and in 12:17; 19:10; and 20:4 the testimony given by Christians. In 19:10 this testimony of Jesus is identified as "the Spirit of prophecy," so that those who give it stand in the company of God's servants the prophets (cf. 22:9).
83. Cf. I Kings 17:1; Luke 4:25; James 5:17.
84. Cf. II Kings 1:10ff.
85. The explicit prophetic identity of the figures equated with the two olive trees, as well as the two lampstands, in Revelation 11:3, 4 confirms the conclusion that the two "sons of oil" in Zechariah 4, who are there equated with the two olive trees and more specifically with the end-boughs, are to be interpreted as prophets rather than as priests and kings.

peoples, nations, languages, and kings. The prophetic character of his task is also brought out by the motif of the eating of the book (vv. 8-10), which is drawn from the experience of the prophet Ezekiel.[86] The witness character of the Angel-Lord is also conspicuous. He stands as witness in oath posture and, affirming continuity with the tradition of God's "servants the prophets" (v. 7), prophesies the finishing of the mystery of God. In effect, then, the commissioning of the apostle-witness by the Angel-Witness is a fashioning of the apostle in the prophetic image of his Lord.

After the apostle-witness has received the prophet commission (Rev. 10), that commission is extended to the church as a whole (Rev. 11). The stamp of apostolic prophethood is placed on the entire church by depicting it by the symbol of the two witnesses (lampstands), who possess the prerogatives and powers of prophet-apostles. The parallel between the church of Revelation 11 and the apostle of Revelation 10 includes the universal extent of the mission in each case, as well as the common function of witnessing with authoritative power. The two witnesses must carry through to completion the world-commission given to the apostle-seer (Rev. 10:11). It is in the sequel of their mission, described in Revelation 11:9 in terms echoing the universal commission of John in Revelation 10:11, that its world-wide scope becomes evident. Tragic though its effect was, their mission reached the peoples and tribes and languages and nations of those who dwell on earth. Moreover, when the theme of the anger of the nations against the two witnesses and their resurrection-vindication by the Lord is taken up into the chapter's concluding doxology, the persecuted-rewarded church symbolized by the two witnesses is identified as God's "servants the prophets" (Rev. 11:18).

The line of prophetic continuity can thus be traced back from the church (Rev. 11:18) through the apostle's commission (Rev. 10:11) to the commissioning Angel-Lord who took his stand in the tradition of God's "servants the prophets" (Rev. 10:7). It is, in fact, the Angel-prophet of Revelation 10 who gives the two-witness church of Revelation 11 its great commission (v. 3). For the opening verses of chapter eleven are a continuation of the Angel's instructions to John begun in

---

86. Cf. Ezekiel 3:1-3.

chapter ten. In sum then, the scenario of the whole Revelation 10 and 11 complex is taken over from the Old Testament model of the Angel-prophet directing the prophets, fashioning them in their covenantal office in his own prophet-likeness. Under this figure of the Angel, the Apocalypse portrays Christ structuring the apostle-church in his prophetic image.

Before the Lord proceeds to produce his image in his church as a whole (Rev. 11) he forms the apostle-seer in his prophetic likeness (Rev. 10). This symbolic sequence in the Apocalypse reflects the distinctive phasing of new covenant history with its foundational age of the apostles. That opening period witnessed a special reenactment of the Old Testament drama of creation in the prophet-likeness of the Angel. Corresponding to the Spirit-Presence, the Angel, and the Moses-prophets were the Spirit-Paraclete, Christ, and the apostles. Like the true prophet, who was certified by beholding the divine Glory in the heavenly council, the true apostle must be a witness of the glory of Christ. And as the prophets could fulfill their office only as they were sent forth with a Spirit-qualification that transformed them into a likeness of the Angel-prophet, himself the revelation of the Glory-Presence, so it was with the apostles. Their entrance upon their mission of witness to the peoples, nations, languages, and kings, which was to be in demonstration of the Spirit and power, must await the promised presence of another Paraclete (John 14:16), the Spirit-Paraclete, who was with Jesus a prophet-paradigm for the apostles, for he was sent as a witness to Christ (John 14:26; 15:26), convicting of sin and righteousness and judgment (John 16:7–11).

This special pneumatic experience of the apostles was another intimation, along with the similar experience of the Old Testament prophets, of how the entire church founded on Christ and the apostles will at last participate in the image of God in its consummated form. That consummation of the story of the *imago Dei* is the subject of the closing vision of the Book of Revelation, which is the final passage we have selected to illustrate the use of the prophetic model of the image of God.

The introduction to this vision is marked by the last appearance in the book of the statement that John was "in the Spirit" (21:10). This phrase appears earlier at Revelation 1:10; 4:2; and 17:3 and describes the experience of rapture into the Glory realm, the prophetic-apostolic foretaste of the eschatological perfecting of the *imago Dei*. John "in the Spirit" in Revelation 1 stands in the presence of the Glory embodied in the Son of Man. In Revelation 4, John's "in the Spirit" experience (v. 2a) answers to the invitation to come up into heaven (v. 1), the unveiling of which reveals God enthroned in the midst of the unceasing praise of the hosts of the Glory council (vv. 2ff). In Revelation 17, John "in the Spirit" is escorted by an angel member of the heavenly court to see a vision of the harlot Babylon, which is a foil for the closing vision of the bride Jerusalem. Then in Revelation 21, John "in the Spirit" is again conducted by one of the heavenly assembly, this time to see the church of the consummation, and he discovers that there in the New Jerusalem all God's people are "in the Spirit."

For John sees a new world in which the cloud veil that had hidden the heavenly realm of God in his council from the eyes of mortal men is gone. Not only does the horizontal demarcation between the old temple and city disappear in the New Jerusalem, but the vertical distinction between heavenly and earthly temples as well. The temple-city's height, great as its length and breadth, encompasses the heavens. Cuboid New Jerusalem is thus a cosmic holy of holies. It is none other than the archetypal heavenly court of the divine council. Entrée into the council that had been the peculiar privilege of prophets and apostles caught up in the Spirit is now the normal joy of everyone, and so the longing of Moses is fulfilled: all the Lord's people are prophets—in the Spirit.

Previously we observed that features of the priestly Glory-vestments are woven into the description of the adornment of the New Jerusalem-bride.[87] But the prophetic model also makes its contribution to this symbolic portrait of the perfected beauty of God's Glory-likeness in his people. If New Jerusalem is clothed in priestly vestments, it is also covered with the prophet's mantle.[88]

The foundations of the city walls bear the names of the apostle-prophets (21:14) and at the gates of the city stand angel-prophets

---

87. See p. 49.
88. Compare the witness-church clothed in sackcloth in Revelation 11:3. Cf. II Kings 1:8; Isaiah 20:2; Zechariah 13:4; Mark 1:6.

(21:12).[89] The presence of the angels is an index of the identity of this cosmic holy of holies as the heavenly court of the council, a feature that belongs to the prophetic model since, though the Israelite high-priest entered the earthly holy of holies, only the prophets in the Spirit entered the heavenly holy of holies, the Spirit-realm. Another distinctly prophetic feature of the New Jerusalem is the identification of its citizens as God's "servants" (22:3), for in the Book of Revelation that title is predominantly, if not consistently, an equivalent of "prophet."[90] Moreover, these "servants" are described as enjoying the kind of prophetic experience Moses had: "they shall see his face; and his name shall be in their foreheads" (22:4). Commenting on this verse earlier,[91] we noted the equivalence of the divine name and glory, and thus the allusion to Moses' luminous countenance. Not only are all God's people to be prophets, but they are all to share in the highest level of prophetic intimacy with God and of transfigured prophetic likeness to the divine Glory.

Since the Spirit-rapture of the prophets was a pneumatic foretaste of entrance into the ultimate glorified form of the image of God, it was especially appropriate that the prophetic model of the royal priestly glory of the *imago Dei* should inform the symbolism of a vision like that of the New Jerusalem in Revelation 21 and 22. But even the prophetic model does not suffice to portray the glory of the new mankind re-created in the image of God in Christ Jesus. The relationship of Jesus, the divine paradigm prophet, to his image-bearing prophet-church of the new covenant involves a union beyond anything that obtained in the relationship between the Old Testament Angel-prophet and the Old Testament prophets fashioned in his likeness. The Lord

---

89. Cf. Isaiah 62:6.

90. In 1:1 (cf. 22:6, 9), the "servants" are those, like God's "servant John," the prophet-seer himself, who receive the prophetic revelation of this book from "the Lord God of the holy prophets." In chapters ten and eleven, where the prophet theme is pervasive, we find the explicit combination "(God's) servants the prophets" (10:7; 11:18). In 15:3 it is the paradigm prophet, Moses, who is called "the servant of God." The "servants" of 19:2, 5 are the "prophets" of 18:24. There is probably an allusion to the false prophets opposed to Elijah in the seduced "servants" of the "prophetess" Jezebel in 2:20. On the sealed "servants of our God" in 7:3, see the comments on 22:3, 4 above.

91. See pp. 54f.

Jesus and the church created in his image in the Spirit are identified with each other in the mystery of the union of the Head and the body. There is an intimation of this identification in Revelation 11:4 when the two witnesses are identified not only with the lampstand of Zechariah 4 but with the olive trees, the Source of the Spirit-oil. Christ's presence in the midst of his seven lampstand-witness churches (Rev. 1:12, 13) as he gives his witness through them[92] is a distinguishable but inseparable presence.

Great indeed is this mystery of the oneness of Christ and his church, yet a mystery with an analogue in the union of the man and his wife.[93] And this marriage model also contributes, in fact, more plainly so than the priestly or prophetic models, to the symbolism of the church consummated in the image of God at the close of the Apocalypse. Scrutiny of the details does indeed disclose that the adornment of the heavenly city is a priest's vestments and a prophet's mantle, but it is expressly the adornment of the bride made ready for the marriage of the Lamb (Rev. 19:7; 21:2, 9). As the bride, the glory-image of her husband, is one flesh with him, so the church re-created as Christ's Glory-image, is one body with the Lord, her Head, in the Spirit.

---

92. See footnote 82.
93. Cf. Ephesians 5:30–32.

Chapter Four

The Spirit-Presence and His Parousia-*Day*

Images of the Glory-Spirit other than his human image have come to our attention as we have followed the theme of the *imago Dei* through the Bible. One such replica of the Glory-cloud was the cosmos itself, conceptualized as a vast temple of God. Some other images of the Glory will be mentioned in the present chapter. But our investigation here will center on the Glory as the divine Presence, or *parousia,* particularly on the Sabbath phase of this theophanic Presence, and we shall be taking notice of prototypal images of that Sabbath-Omega phase of the Glory-Spirit.

Primal *Parousia*

Genesis 3:8 describes the approach of the Lord God following the fateful disobedience of the man and the woman in the garden. Judgment was the purpose of God's coming and he proceeded at once to prosecute his lawsuit against the covenant-breakers and to pronounce the damnation of their tempter.

How then are we to picture this coming of the Lord? One would expect that the theophany would have been fashioned to express the ominous design of the divine mission. Customary renderings of Genesis 3:8a do not convey such an impression, however. The familiar version of it, ''and they heard the voice of the Lord God walking in the garden in the cool of the day,'' suggests something rather more casual. It is our hope to show here that the kind of epiphany that the historical situation calls for is what the original text actually does depict—an advent of the Lord in his awesomely fearful judicial Glory. And if so, Genesis 3:8 turns out to be an account of a primal *parousia,* a record of the beginnings of what is known later in the Scriptures as the day of the Lord.

The exegesis of Genesis 3:8 to be recommended here emerged in connection with the development of the interpretation of "the Spirit" in Genesis 1:2 as the Shekinah-Glory[1] and the identification of this Glory-Spirit as the specific referent in the creation of man in God's image (Gen. 1:26 and 2:7) and as the sheltering divine Presence over the holy garden in Eden.[2] That reading of Genesis 1 and 2 prepared for the recognition of the theophanic Glory elsewhere in this context, and the discovery of such an additional instance of this theophanic phenomenon—in Genesis 3:8—serves in turn to confirm our earlier identification of the Glory-Spirit.

The Voice of Yahweh

"They heard the voice *(qôl)* of Yahweh God" (Gen. 3:8a). It is generally agreed that the "voice" here is not that of the Lord's speaking, as though he was heard conversing or calling. It is rather the "voice," or sound, of the Lord's coming that was heard.[3] In other passages *qôl* is used for the sound of approaching feet.[4] The sound in Genesis 3:8, however, is not that of mere footsteps.[5] This passage must be played fortissimo. What Adam and Eve heard was frighteningly loud. It was the shattering thunder of God's advent in judgment.

One of the prominent aspects of theophany throughout the Old Testament is its distinctive sound. Sometimes this sound is called "the voice of Yahweh" or "his voice."[6] Instances of this phenomenon of the clarion identifying sound of the divine Presence, or *parousia,* are found in historical narrative, in accounts of the visionary experience of the seers, and in poetic descriptions of God's presence and action in the world, whether reflections on the past or apocalyptic portrayals of future judgments.

There was that day at Sinai that Israel must carry in memory (Deut. 4:9, 10), the day that dawned with lightnings and thunders *(qôlôṯ)*, the day when the mountain burned with a fire enveloped in theophanic

---

1. See pp. 13ff.
2. See pp. 35ff.
3. The subject of the participle *miṯhallēḵ* is Yahweh God, not *qôl*, and the sound is the sound of God (cf. "your sound," v. 10). Yet it is the sound of the motion of God's approaching that was heard and in effect the sound too moved across the garden.
4. See I Kings 14:6 and II Kings 6:32.
5. "Walking" is a misleadingly imprecise translation of *miṯhallēḵ*. See further below.
6. See Psalm 18:13(14); Isaiah 30:31; Jeremiah 25:30; Joel 3:16.

clouds, for Yahweh came down in fire on the top of the mountain and the whole mountain quaked (Exod. 19:16–18; Deut. 4:11). Specifically, Israel must not forget that they saw no anthropomorphous or other kind of form on that day—"there was only *qôl*" (Deut. 4:12), as the voice of the trumpet sounded louder and louder and God spoke with thundering voice, declaring his covenant (Exod. 19:19; Deut. 4:13, 33; 5:4, 22; cf. Heb. 12:18f., 25f.).

There was also that later theophany at Horeb witnessed by Elijah, which so remarkably paralleled the experience of Moses at Sinai, and here again the greatest possible emphasis is given to the theophanic *qôl*. According to the traditional understanding of I Kings 19:12, what Elijah heard was "a still small voice," in which case this would be an atypical instance of the sound associated with theophany. But *ql dmmh dqh* may be better rendered "a roaring, crushing voice (sound),"[7] and the insistence of this passage is that while wind, earthquake, and fire accompany the Presence, the Lord is peculiarly identified with the thunderous *qôl*.[8]

Another historical narrative in which God's presence is said to have been made known by the sound of his movement in the midst of his heavenly armies is the account of David's battle against the Philistines in the Valley of Rephaim. On that occasion David's advance on earth was matched by (or better, corresponded to) Yahweh's advance above,[9] the latter signalized by the "voice" of marching[10] over the tree-tops (II Sam. 5:24).[11]

New Testament Pentecost may also be mentioned here with its coming of the Spirit as divine Witness to seal the new covenant, a counter-

---

7. This is argued convincingly by J. Lust, "A Gentle Breeze or a Roaring Thunderous Sound?," *Vetus Testamentum* 25 (1975): 110–15. In I Kings 19:13, *qôl* refers to God's voice in challenging question. Note the structural similarity between the accounts of the encounter and dialogue in this passage and in Genesis 3:8ff.

8. The point then might well be to reaffirm the emphasis of Exodus 34:5ff. and Deuteronomy 4:12f.: God is not apprehended in the visible and palpable, but reveals himself in the covenant word of the Spirit, proclaiming his sovereign name.

9. Battle scenes in royal Assyrian reliefs depict human king below and divine king above in identical warrior-posture.

10. The noun (*ṣeʿādāh*) that defines *qôl* here is from the verb *ṣʿd* "step, march," which belongs to the Sinai-conquest theophany tradition (cf. Judg. 5:4; Ps. 68:7[8]; Hab. 3:12). The verb *yṣʾ* used with *ṣeʿādāh* in II Samuel 5:24 appears as a parallel to *ṣʿd* in each of these other passages.

11. Cf. also I Samuel 7:10.

part to the Spirit's descent on Sinai as the Glory-Witness to the old covenant.[12] Once again, along with the fire as a sign of the Spirit's presence there was the sound[13] from heaven, a roaring storm-like noise. The ancient Glory theophany was adapted to this new time after Christ's incarnation and glorification, but the mighty voice was still a major feature among the insignia of the Presence.

Ezekiel's accounts of his ecstatic visionary experiences provide the most elaborate biblical treatment of the Glory theophany. As perceived by the prophet, it was a cherubim-propelled chariot with the Glory-figure enthroned above a firmament above the cherubim. Such was the hidden reality that was disclosed to him from within what he first caught sight of as a great cloud coming out of the north, driven by the storm-wind and bright with an inner flashing fire (Ezek. 1:4ff.). Impressed by the sound as well as the sight of the phenomenon, Ezekiel reports: "When they [the cherubim] went, I heard the *qôl* of their wings, like the *qôl* of many waters, like the *qôl* of the Almighty, the *qôl* of tumult like the *qôl* of an army. . . . And there came a *qôl* from the firmament above their heads. . . . Such was the appearance of the likeness of the glory of Yahweh. And when I saw it, I fell upon my face, and I heard the *qôl* of one speaking" (Ezek. 1:24, 25a, 28b). When describing further appearances of the Glory to him, Ezekiel continues to mention the impressive sound that accompanied it. Attributing the sound again to the moving of the wings of the cherubim and the turning of the wheels (3:13; 10:5), he compares it to the noise of earthquake (3:12) and once more to the voice of the Almighty when he speaks (10:5) and to the sound of many waters (43:2). Of particular interest for Genesis 3:8 is the theophany episode recorded in Ezekiel 9–11, for it is strongly evocative of the Genesis 3 event. Here again the Glory moves in judgment against those who have defiled God's sanctuary[14] and the offenders are driven out (11:9ff.) while the cherubim-guardians are positioned on the east of the holy city (11:22, 23).

Other seers also remark upon the mighty sound that attended their visionary encounters with the Glory of the Lord. They liken it to the

---

12. See pp. 19f.

13. The noun *êchos* used here is found in the description of the Sinai theophany in Hebrews 12:19 with reference to the sounding of the trumpet spoken of in Exodus 19:16 (where the LXX uses the verb *êcheô*).

14. Cf. Ezekiel 43:3.

sound of a multitude of people or the sound of many waters, and they note that it produced the effect of quaking in all about.[15]

In poetic accounts, the natural and theophanic cloud formations merge, the former being viewed as an extension of the latter so that the inner reality of the theophany becomes the poetic explanation of the natural phenomena. Thus, just as Ezekiel accounts for the roar of the storm wind from the north in terms of the movement of the wings of the cherubim, so biblical poetry elsewhere interprets the noise of thunder in terms of Yahweh giving forth his voice. Indeed, this identification of the voice of the Lord with thunder is found in passages that speak of the manifestation of God's power in both the ordinary storms of nature[16] and in extraordinary theophanic and eschatological storm phenomena.[17] The prominence of the sound element among the theophanic phenomena is especially evident in Psalm 29, which is a sustained celebration of Yahweh's *qôl* (vv. 3-9).[18] As we shall observe further below, the *qôl yhwh* is an important element in the prophetic portrayal of the day of Yahweh.

Whether it is the sound of the advancing Glory or the sound of the Lord's speaking from the midst of the Glory, the *qôl yhwh* is characteristically loud, arrestingly loud. It is likened to the crescendo of ocean and storm, the rumbling roar of earthquake. It is the noise of war, the trumpeting of signal horns and the din of battle.[19] It is the thunder of the storm-chariot of the warrior-Lord, coming in judgments that convulse creation and confound the kings of the nations.[20]

Such a conception of the *qôl yhwh* clearly fits the Genesis 3:8

---

15. See Isaiah 6:4-6; Daniel 10:6f.; Revelation 1:15.

16. See, e.g., Job 37:4,5; Psalms 29:3ff.; 104:7; Jeremiah 10:13.

17. See, e.g., Psalms 46:6(7); 68:33(34); Isaiah 30:30; cf. Psalm 18:13(14).

18. Since thunder is similarly spoken of in the Ugaritic texts as "the voice of Baal" *(ql b^c l)*, a hymn like Psalm 29, whose terminology in general recalls Canaanite texts, was probably designed, for one thing at least, for the polemic purpose of rejecting Baal's claims in favor of Yahweh's with respect to lordship over creation and nature's storms. On this Psalm's reflection of the motif of the seven thunders, attributed to Baal in a Ugaritic text, see J. Day, "Echoes of Baal's Seven Thunders and Lightnings in Psalm XXIX and Habakkuk III 9 and the Identity of the Seraphim in Isaiah VI," *Vetus Testamentum* 29 (1979): 143ff. Cf. Revelation 10:3, 4.

19. Cf., e.g., II Samuel 5:24; Isaiah 30:30ff.; Joel 2:11; 3:11, 16; Zephaniah 1:14. Similarly, Baal's identity as the thunderer is related to his role as a divine warrior. In the cuneiform literature of Mesopotamia too the epiphany of warrior gods is accompanied by a frightening thunder or roar.

20. Cf., e.g., Psalms 18:9, 10, 13 (10, 11, 14); 47:5(6); 68:33; 104:3, 7; Isaiah 30:27,

situation very well. There too the "voice" of Yahweh is the sound of divine advent. The verb used for God's approach *(mithallēk)* is used elsewhere for the activity of the Glory-Presence among the Israelites.[21] In Psalm 104:3, in context with a reference to the thunder-sound of God (v. 7), this verb (in the Pi'el) denotes the procession of God, mounted on his wind-driven cloud-chariot. The Hithpa'el of this verb is used to describe the movement of agents of the divine council, which is found within the Glory-cloud, when they are on missions of surveillance and judgment.[22] It also describes God himself engaged in surveillance.[23] Similarly, the purpose of the coming of the Lord denoted by this verb in Genesis 3:8 was to execute judgment. And the "voice" of Yahweh that signalized this coming was a terror going before him, driving the guilty pair into hiding from the Face of their Maker (Gen. 3:8b).[24] This advent recorded in Genesis 3:8 thus corresponds fully in its purpose and effect to the awesome approach of the Glory met with elsewhere in Scripture, the approach with which a thunderous voice of Yahweh is regularly associated. There is every reason, therefore, to perceive God's movement through the garden in Genesis 3 as an advent in the terrible judicial majesty of his Glory theophany and to hear "the voice" that heralded this advent as the characteristic theophanic thunder.

The Spirit of the Day

How the traditional understanding of Genesis 3:8a has managed to maintain itself in the face of what rather obviously must be the point of

---

30; Ezekiel 1:24; 43:2.
21. Leviticus 26:12; Deuteronomy 23:14(15); II Samuel 7:6, 7. It is used in the Qal for the Spirit and the living creatures in Ezekiel 1 and 10 and for the Angel of the Lord in Genesis 18:33 and Judges 6:21. The Qal with *lpny* is used frequently for the divine vanguard on the way from Egypt to Canaan, variously identified as Yahweh, the Angel, and the pillar of the cloud (Exod. 13:21; 14:19; 23:23; Num. 14:14; Deut. 1:30,33; 20:4; 31:8; cf. Isa. 45:2; 52:12; 58:8).
22. Job 1:7; 2:2; Zechariah 1:10, 11; 6:7; cf. Genesis 5:22, 24; 6:9; 18:22.
23. Job 22:14. Eliphaz imputes to Job (unfairly) the sentiment that God, by reason of the thick clouds about his heavenly dwelling, cannot see what is happening on earth (vv. 13,14a) but walks about (i.e., surveys) only the vault of heaven (v. 14b). Possibly Eliphaz is comparing Job to Adam, who supposed he might hide from God. Note the apparent allusion to prediluvian world history immediately afterwards (vv. 15ff.).
24. Cf. Judges 5:5; Psalm 68:2, 8(3,9).

the statement in its context may be accounted for by the difficulty encountered in the adverbial phrase *lrwḥ hyywm* (AV, "in the cool of the day"). Starting from the relative obscurity of this phrase, which is not found elsewhere in the Bible, traditional exegesis has been led away from the natural meaning of the first part of the sentence. But if we follow the sound exegetical practice of proceeding from what is clear to what is obscure, it will appear that *lrwḥ hyywm*, though cryptically concise, is actually an eloquent addition to this verse's description of the advent of the Glory.

Certainly the customary temporal rendering of *lrwḥ hyywm* has its problems, quite apart from any grammatical questions arising from the preposition (*l-*). Why, one wonders, would so simple and ordinary an idea as that of "evening" be expressed by a phrase at once so rare[25] and ambiguous.[26] And what would be the point of such a temporal reference? Are we really prepared to accept the anthropomorphism of the Lord's seeking the relief that might be afforded by the evening air from the burden of the day? Moreover, on such an interpretation, the purpose assigned to this excursion bears only an incidental relation to what God actually proceeded to do. The momentous primeval judgment would then have transpired just coincidentally to what began as an idyllic stroll.[27]

Understandably, numerous commentators, uneasy with the prevalent view, have sought for a more satisfactory exegesis, some through textual emendation. As alternatives to the temporal view of the prepositional phrase, local and modal interpretations have been suggested, some giving *rûᵃḥ* its lexical value of "quarter, direction" and others

---

25. Cf. e.g., *lᵉʿēṭ'ereḇ* in Genesis 8:11; 24:11; etc.

26. "The wind (*rûᵃḥ*) of the day" might be an oppressive hot wind (Job 37:17; Jer. 4:11; Ezek. 17:10; 19:12; Hos. 12:1; 13:15; Jonah 4:8) rather than a cool evening breeze.

27. U. Cassuto, *A Commentary on the Book of Genesis* (Jerusalem: the Magnes Press, 1961), pp. 152ff., offers an alternate temporal interpretation that has the merit of showing concern for the context. He reads *rwḥ* as cognate to an Arabic and Ugaritic verb denoting action that takes place in the afternoon and he takes *hayyôm* as referring to the very day Adam and Eve sinned. The point is then that the threat of Genesis 2:17 did not fail (though Cassuto himself does not understand *bᵉyôm* in Genesis 2:17 in such literal terms). Calvin (see his commentary on Genesis, *in loc.*), though translating *rwḥ* as "wind," senses that God gave with this wind some extraordinary symbol of his presence.

understanding it as the "wind" and regarding it as the source of the sound mentioned earlier in the verse. It is not our purpose to rehearse and assess in detail challenges to the traditional view presented hitherto, none of which has gained notable acceptance anyway, but to pursue the new possibilities opened by our interpretation of the earlier part of Genesis 3:8a.

As previously mentioned, there are references to the Glory theophany in the context surrounding Genesis 3:8 (Gen. 1:2, 26; 2:7; 3:22ff.), and this theophany is, moreover, called "the Spirit $(rû^ah)$ of God" in Genesis 1:2. We are thus alerted to the possibility of a similar usage of $rû^ah$ in Genesis 3:8. And if, as interpreted above, the words in this verse which are qualified by the phrase *lrwh hyywm* themselves refer to the Glory theophany on a mission of judgment, the identification of the $rû^ah$ here as the divine Spirit, the Glory-Spirit, is quite compelling.

In keeping with this identification of $rû^ah$ as the Spirit in the judgment context of Genesis 3:8, we find that the divine Spirit is closely linked with the function of divine judgment elsewhere in Scripture too. Of primary importance is the fact that "Spirit" appears as the designation of the Glory-chariot, the Presence of God in sovereign power on judicial missions of surveillance, sentencing, and execution.[28] But in addition to those instances where the theophanic Glory is the Spirit's vehicle of judgment are the cases where the Spirit comes upon human agents of divine judgment as an empowering endowment.

God's Spirit thus came upon those who were raised up to be "judges" of his people. The first instance mentioned in the Book of Judges is characteristic. The Spirit of Yahweh came on Othniel "and he judged Israel" (Judg. 3:10), that is, he became the agent of God's judicial action in behalf of Israel, going to war and delivering them from the oppression of Cushan-rishathaim.[29] Of his Servant, God declared: "I have put my Spirit on him; he shall bring forth judgment to the nations" (Isa. 42:1), and the Servant himself claims this Spirit-endowment to carry out the task of the day of God's vindication of his people (Isa. 61:1ff.). What is thus affirmed of the Servant of the Lord

---

28. On the designating of the Glory theophany as "Spirit," see p. 15 and below.
29. Cf. Judges 6:34; 11:29; 14:19; 15:14, 20; I Samuel 11:6; 16:13.

answers to the prophecy concerning the messianic Branch of the royal line of the son of Jesse: the Spirit of Yahweh will rest upon him (Isa. 11:1, 2) for his work of judging the meek of the earth and slaying the wicked (Isa. 11:3ff.). Similarly, in Isaiah 28 the prophet speaks of a day of judgment in which the Lord of hosts will be a Glory-crown to a remnant-people and a "Spirit of judgment" for those who occupy the tribunal (vv. 5, 6). Lying behind all this is Isaiah's eschatological picture of Jerusalem as a perfected remnant-community, purged by "the Spirit of judgment and by the Spirit of burning," the theophanic Spirit-cloud that will also cover the restored Zion as a canopy of glory (Isa. 4:4–6).[30]

On our understanding of Genesis 3:8, its identification of the divine agent in the first great divine judgment in human history as "the Spirit of the day" is a fontal revelation of the Spirit's judicial function. When this theme emerges later in Scripture, there is at times an apparently quite direct allusion to Genesis 3:8. Psalm 139, for example, brings to mind at once the circumstances of Genesis 3, as the psalmist asks: "Where could I go from your Spirit or where flee from your Presence?" (v. 7). When he confesses that if one were concealed in the darkness of Sheol, the very light of God's shining Spirit-Presence would make the night like day, exposing the hidden one to plain sight (v. 12), he clearly evokes the guilty pair hiding in the shadows among the trees of the garden of Eden, yet for all their desperate efforts exposed by the coming of the Spirit of the day (Gen. 3:9ff.).

Instead of using the designation "Spirit of judgment" *(mišpāṭ)*, Genesis 3:8a calls him the "Spirit of the day." We shall want to reflect on the equivalency of the concepts of the day and judgment, but it will be well first to consider how the sentence as a whole might best be read. What, we must ask, is the meaning of the preposition (*l-*) in *lrwḥ?* On the present interpretation an answer is readily supplied by the preposition's lexical value of "as," which in various contexts may mean "in the capacity of" or "for the purpose of."

A few illustrations of this usage, all involving the Glory-cloud and the heavenly council, will be useful. Numbers 22 narrates how the Angel of the Lord went and stationed himself in Balaam's way "as an

---

30. See p. 36. Note the expression "the eyes of his glory" in Isaiah 3:8.

adversary'' (*l^esāṭān;* vv. 22, 32). Isaiah says of the messianic scion of
David on whom the Spirit would rest, enabling him to judge the earth
(Isa. 11:1ff.), that "in that day . . . [he] shall stand as a banner *(l^enēs)*
for the peoples; the nations shall rally to him and his royal resting place
shall be [the] Glory'' (v. 10). Using the imagery of a second exodus,
the prophet depicts the Davidic king as an incarnation of the Glory-
cloud which led Israel out of Egypt, functioning as a rallying ensign or
battle standard.[31] An example involving the noun *rûᵃh* is found in II
Chronicles 18:21. For the undoing of Ahab, an angel in the divine
council offers to go and function "as a spirit of falsehood" *(l^erûᵃh
šeqer)* in the mouth of Ahab's prophets.[32] Very similar to the expression "as the Spirit of the day" in Genesis 3:8 is an instance in the
Isaiah 28 passage cited previously: "In that day Yahweh of hosts will
be present . . . as the Spirit of judgment" *(l^erûᵃh mišpāṭ;* vv. 5a, 6a).
In the related vision of the re-created Jerusalem in Isaiah 4, the Glory-
cloud (called in verse 4 "the Spirit of judgment and burning") is said
to serve "as a shade . . . and as a refuge and as a hiding place"
(l^eṣēl . . . ûl^emaḥseh ûl^emistôr; v. 6).[33]

We may then translate Genesis 3:8a: "They heard the sound of
Yahweh God traversing the garden as the Spirit of the day." The
frightening noise of the approaching Glory theophany told them that
God was coming to enter into judgment with them. The sound of
judgment day preceded the awesome sight of the *parousia* of their
Judge. It was evidently heard from afar before the searching, exposing
beams of the theophanic light pierced through the trees in the midst of
the garden. Momentarily, then, it seemed to them possible to hide from
the eyes of Glory among the shadows of the foliage. Thus, inadver-
tently, they positioned themselves at the place of judgment in the garden, at the site of the tree of judicial discernment between good and evil.

The Day of the Spirit

If Genesis 3:8 had read "the *rûᵃh* of judgment" rather than "the
rûᵃh of the day," the course of exegesis would have gotten on the

---

31. For the name-banner aspect of the Glory-cloud see further below.
32. Consider together this passage and Genesis 3:1ff. and Numbers 22:28ff.
33. The redemptive irony emerges here that the concealing shadows and covert which
the guilty pair in Eden sought are available in the very Glory-Presence from which they
futilely fled when that Glory-Spirit approached as the Spirit of burning judgment.

right track much more readily. But once we do discern what the text is saying and see that "the day" must signify judgment, the expression *lrwh hyywm* strikes us as having a very familiar biblical ring to it after all. For eschatological passages of the Bible in both Testaments teem with references to the day of the Lord, that day, the great day, the day of wrath, the day of visitation, etc. If we came upon *rwh hyywm* in some later prophetic context, we would probably catch the judgment meaning of "the day" at once. It is just that we had not expected to encounter this terminology of the day of judgment at this early point in the biblical record.[34]

Now, however, we face the problem of accounting for the emergence of "the day" with judicial connotation in Genesis 3:8. If we do not want to regard the expression as a later, rather inept glossing of an earlier narrative source, we must ask whether there is anything in the immediately antecedent context of Genesis 3:8 that would explain the appearance of "the day" in this verse in a conceptual bond with "the Spirit" and freighted with judicial significance. To raise this question will, we believe, prove to be of considerable heuristic value for the meaning of the Genesis Prologue, in which, it would appear, the answer to our question lies. And what we will find is that it is not Genesis 3:8 but more precisely the creation record that is the ultimately fontal source of the judgment reality which the Scriptures call "the day of the Lord." The Genesis Prologue is the original matrix in which the visual and conceptual shape of that day was first set.

Spirit and day are brought into clear and close conjunction right at the beginning of Genesis 1 in the record of the first day of creation. Though not lying so obviously on the surface, a most significant relationship also obtains between the Spirit and the seventh day. It will in fact appear that the seven-day pattern of the creation record as a whole was so constructed that while it was figuratively indicating the temporal dimension and especially the sabbatical structuring of the creation history,[35] it should also serve as a seven-panelled portrait-paradigm—a prototypal model—of the day of the Lord, which was to

---

34. Typically, in the recent and most comprehensive treatise on the use of the term *day* in the Old Testament, S. J. DeVries, *Yesterday, Today and Tomorrow* (Grand Rapids: Eerdmans, 1975), Genesis 3:8 is not even mentioned.
35. See my "Because It Had Not Rained," *Westminster Theological Journal* 20 (1958): 146–57.

be of such great importance in the unfolding biblical revelation of cosmic-redemptive history.

Immediately after the mention of the Glory-Spirit hovering in the darkness over the deep (Gen. 1:2), the Spirit's[36] creative fiat is introduced: "Let there be light" (v. 3). Then we are at once informed that the Spirit gave to this light, which evidenced his sovereignty over the darkness, the name of "day," *yôm* (v. 5a). It is this day-light *(yôm)* that is definitively characteristic of a day, for a day, as the closing formula of each day-stanza in the creation narrative brings out, is also named *yôm, pars pro toto* after the day-light (vv. 5b, 8b, 13b, etc.).[37] In this initial conjunction of the Spirit and day, day (in its nature as day-light) is seen to be a replication of the Glory-Spirit, which is itself, visually, light—the luminosity of the radiant Shekinah.[38] Henceforth, *yôm* carries with it as it is used for the day of judgment—as already in Genesis 3:8—its original identification with day-light. Accordingly, the imagery of the day of judgment is at times that of sunrise bringing the light of God's Glory from the east.[39] The "day" designation for divine judgment highlights the illuminating judicial penetration of the darkness by the light of the eyes of God, which are their own search-beams, for they are "like a flame of fire."[40]

What we read of the Spirit and the day in the creation record of day one, the definitive day, would be sufficient by itself to account for the expression *lrwḥ hyywm* in Genesis 3:8. For day one identifies the Creator-*rûᵃḥ* as the Creator-Lord of the *yôm* and the *yôm* as a creature-image of the divine Glory-*rûᵃḥ;* and further, the characteriza-

---

36. Though "Spirit of God" is abbreviated to "God" through the remainder of the creation account, the reality denoted by *rûᵃḥ* in Genesis 1:2 is to be understood as in view throughout, as the emergence of the divine council usage in Genesis 1:26 shows. See pp. 22f.

37. The concept *day* here is thus not starkly temporal-quantitative but is filled with an identifying quality.

38. See II Corinthians 4:6 for a biblical allusion to the Spirit's production of light at the creation as a prototype of later divine action, specifically of the redemptive illumination of men by the glory-light of the Lord, the Spirit. Note the Glory-Spirit theme in the broader context of II Corinthians 3-5.

39. See, e.g., Psalm 19:4ff; Ezekiel 43:2; Zechariah 14:7; Malachi 4:1, 2 (3:19, 20); Romans 13:12; II Peter 1:19.

40. Revelation 1:14. This is a description of Christ as the Glory-Spirit incarnate. See pp. 24f. and 48f. On the primal light and judgment, compare also John 1:5 and 3:19.

tion of the *yôm* there prepares for its appearance in Genesis 3:8 with the connotation of the (day-)light of judicial exposure.

But the prototypal concept of the day of the Spirit begun in day one is filled out by the record of the other creation days. Viewed as a whole this day-paradigm is found to contain a complex of the elements that are most conspicuous in the later revelation of the day of the Lord. For in the Genesis Prologue, the day of the Spirit is a time when God takes action[41] and pronounces an assessment. The former is a prominent feature in every day-stanza, and we need only note the equally obvious fact that the divine action is creative action, by which the heaven and earth and all their hosts are brought forth.

The second element, the feature of judicial assessment, requires special comment. What is in view here is the refrain: "God saw that it was good."[42] Divine pronouncement, not just casual observation, is the meaning.[43] God, judging his own works in this case, pronounced them good, so signifying that his fiat-decree had been fully executed. Design is evident in the distribution pattern of this judicial refrain. Seven times the declaration resounds, three times in the first triad of days and four in the second triad, twice each in the third and sixth days (one of the marks of their correspondence in the parallelism of the two triads).[44] In the seventh, summarizing occurrence the pronouncement

---

41. The focus on divine intervention and action is particularly sharp in Psalm 118:24 and Malachi 3:17 and 4:3 (3:21), if the correct rendering of the key phrase is "the day when God acts." Note in these contexts the idea of the shining light of God's Glory (Ps. 118:27 and Mal. 4:1, 2 [3:19, 20]).

42. Genesis 1:4, 10, 12, 18, 21, 25, and 31.

43. The discriminating, elective, judgmental force of the verb *rā'āh*, "see," is well attested. Cf., e.g., Exodus 39:43. Of special interest is an instance in the day of the Lord context of Malachi 3. The prophet rebukes the people for their blasphemous calumny that God saw (pronounced) all the evil-doers good (literally, they were "good in the eyes of Yahweh") and for their cynical query, "Where is the God of judgment?" (Mal. 2:17). Then he warns them that in the day when God takes action they will "see between the righteous and the wicked" (Mal. 3:18), distinguishing one from the other easily by the contrasting judgments of ultimate curse or blessing meted out to them by the Lord on the great day.

44. In the second day-stanza this pronouncement is postponed until the bounding of the waters, which begins with the separation of the waters above and below (vv. 6-8), has been completed by the further limitation set on them to make room for the dry land (vv. 9, 10)—a theme treated with special emphasis in biblical reflections on the sovereign might of the Lord.

is heightened to "very good." Seven acts of "seeing" by the Spirit-Creator are recorded, and here, it would seem, is the ultimate source of the imagery of "the seven eyes which are the seven Spirits of God sent forth into all the earth" (Rev. 5:6) on judicial missions,[45] the seven eyes which are seven torches of fire burning before the Glory-throne of judgment (Rev. 4:5).[46] The dominance of the creation theme in the Revelation 4 context[47] strengthens the likelihood of the suggested relationship between the seven judicial eyes of the Spirit and the seven acts of the Spirit's seeing in Genesis 1, and that relationship corroborates the judicial-declarative interpretation of the refrain, "God saw that it was good."

Glory-Spirit and light and divine action, creative and judicial—all these features are present in the paradigmatic day of the Spirit-Lord in the creation Prologue of Genesis. Beyond these there are distinctive elements found in the seventh day of creation and its peculiar relation to the Spirit which fill out the prototypal representation of the eschatological day of the Lord.

"The Glory-Spirit was present at the beginning of creation as a sign of the *telos* of creation, as the Alpha-archetype of the Omega-Sabbath that was the goal of creation history."[48] In our first chapter, that statement introduced an analysis of the function of the Glory-Spirit of Genesis 1:2, showing that it acted as a paradigm-power, reproducing its own temple-likeness in the cosmos and in man, the image of God. Another instance of this, noted above, was the reproduction of the Glory-light in the day-light of day one, and in that connection it may further be observed that the bearers of this light-likeness, the luminaries of day four, sustain a functional likeness to the Spirit. Just as the Spirit, according to day one, manifested his sovereignty by bringing day-light into earth's darkness and separating light from darkness and day from night (Gen. 1:3–5), so the heavenly luminaries, as replicas of the Glory-Spirit, were given the status of rulers, to give

---

45. Cf. II Chronicles 16:9; Ezra 5:5; Zechariah 3:9; 4:10.
46. They are also identified as the seven Spirits. The eyes and the fire are united in the eyes of fire of Revelation 1:14, where they are the eyes of Christ the Spirit-Lord, as also in Revelation 5:6 (cf. above note 40).
47. See especially v. 11.
48. See p. 20.

light on the earth and to separate light from darkness and day from night (Gen. 1:14–18).[49] But at present our interest is especially in that culminating instance of the Spirit-replicating pattern found in the relation between the Alpha-archetype and the seventh day, the Omega-Sabbath.

Within the luminous cloud-veil of the Glory was the enthroned Creator-Judge, and that central throne-reality of the Glory finds its apocalypse in the final, seventh panel of the creation "week." For on the seventh day God rested from his work of creation and this Sabbath of God is a royal resting, an enthronement on the judgment seat. One indication that God's Sabbath-rest consequent to the finishing of his cosmic house was an enthronement is that the Scriptures present the converse of this idea; they portray God's enthronement in his microcosmic (temple-)house as a Sabbath-rest.[50] Thus, when Isaiah makes his challenging comparison between the earthly temple built by Israel and the creation temple of heaven and earth built by God at the beginning, he introduces the Sabbath-rest imagery of the creation history as a parallel to God's throne house: "The heaven is my throne, and the earth is my footstool: Where is the house that ye build unto me? And where is the place of my rest *(m ͤ nûḥāh)?*" (Isa. 66:1; cf. II Chron. 6:18; Acts 7:49).[51]

Isaiah brings together the Spirit and the Sabbath-*m ͤ nûḥāh* in other passages too. Isaiah 63, reflecting on Deuteronomy 32 (which depicts God's leading of Israel in terms of the Glory hovering over creation at the beginning),[52] mentions the Angel of the Glory-Presence as the one who bore Israel (v. 9) and variously denotes the divine Presence as the Holy Spirit or Spirit of the Lord (vv. 10, 11, 14) or as his arm of Glory

---

49. This identity in functional accomplishment of days one and four continues to be an unanswered demonstration of the nonsequential, topical arrangement of the data in the creation account. Cf. note 35 above. That the Glory is paradigmatic for the heavenly lights may be seen further in their identification as "the host of heaven" (e.g., Deut. 4:19; 17:3), corresponding to the hosts of the angels of light, which are conspicuous in the Glory-Spirit of the day. See further below, note 136, and chapter three, note 77.
50. Cf. pp. 20f., 39ff., and 46.
51. The point cannot be pursued here at length. On the conjunction of throne and Sabbath-rest, see I Chronicles 28:2; Psalm 132:7, 8, 13, 14; (cf. Num. 10:35, 36). On the sabbatical connotation of *m ͤ nûḥāh,* cf. Exodus 20:11; Deuteronomy 12:9; I Kings 8:56; Psalm 95:11; Hebrews 4:3, 4, 9.
52. Compare Isaiah 63:9, 10, 16 with Deuteronomy 32:11, 15, 18.

(v. 12; cf. v. 15). And the prophet attributes to the Glory-Spirit the guidance of Israel through the depths of the sea (v. 13; cf. Deut. 32:10; Gen. 1:2) on to the Sabbath-rest in the land of their inheritance: "The Spirit of the Lord brought him to rest" (v. 14; cf. Deut. 12:9). In effect, the prophet says that in the exodus re-creation there was a recapitulation of the role of the Glory-Spirit in creation from Genesis 1:2 to Genesis 2:2.

Elsewhere, Isaiah says there is to be a second exodus re-creation led by the royal Branch on whom the Spirit of the Lord will rest (Isa. 11:1, 2, 11, 15f.). By righteous judgment he will procure the peace of the new creation for the meek of the earth (vv. 2-9; cf. Isa. 61:1ff.; 65:17-25). In this context the prophet states: "In that day there shall be a root of Jesse, who shall stand as a banner for the peoples; the nations shall rally to him and his royal resting place (m^{e}nûḥāh) will be [the] Glory" (v. 10; cf. v. 12). Isaiah thus perceived that the Spirit-Glory not only conducted to the Sabbath, but was itself archetypal of the Sabbath realm of divine enthronement.

Judicial pronouncements accompany the enthronement motif in the seventh day of creation, enhancing the likeness of the seventh day to the Glory on the one hand and its prototypal relation to the final judgment day on the other. We have observed that the refrain "God saw that it was good" imparted to the other days of creation a judicial aspect. After the creation of the human temple-image of the Spirit, this self-assessing process of divine judgment culminated in a final summary-verdict: "God saw everything that he had made, and, behold, it was very good" (Gen. 1:31). This pronouncement was transitional to the Sabbath, indeed, the beginning of the Sabbath. The Sabbath itself is the consummating declaration that creation was finished (Gen. 2:1, 2).[53] This word of the seventh day is like the creative fiats by which God set bounds on the realms of the darkness and the deep, for by it God bounded the period of the six days, closing the age of creation and opening the genealogical times of Adam. But it is also the word of sealing approbation, a declaration of the Creator's

---

53. The pattern of the eschatological day is clearly manifest here. Cf., e.g., Revelation 10:6f. and 11:15.

satisfaction in his works. God's Sabbath celebrates the omnipotence of his creatorhood (Gen. 1:1) and the omniscience of the solution achieved by the Spirit of Genesis 1:2c for the architectural problem posed by the deep-and-darkness of Genesis 1:2a and b. Such was the bounding of the deep and the darkness that they too made positive contributions to the kingdom of life which God had designed for the habitation of man, his image-temple. The pronouncement of the Sabbath was God's word of self-glorifying judgment.

The divine Sabbath was thus a realization in the time field of the judicial sovereignty of God that came to expression in the Glory-Spirit. In the seventh day, the Glory was translated into temporal-eschatological dimensions. The Almighty is accordingly confessed as the One who is, and who was, and who is to come—eternal, unchangeable, yet known from our cosmic perspective as both historical Alpha and historical Omega.[54] Though the divine Sabbath itself is rather a distinctive phase of the Glory than a replica of it, the Creator did produce, preceptively, a replica of the Glory when he instituted the human Sabbath (Gen. 2:3). The weekly Sabbath is a copy of the Glory temporally translated as the sabbatical day of the Lord. It thus appears that the Genesis Prologue closes in Genesis 2:3 with an explicit instance of the recurring feature of the reproduction of the Glory-Spirit paradigm, a reproduction of the Spirit of the day in a symbolic day of the Spirit.

Further, the seventh day, the divine Sabbath itself, *is* the day of the Lord. Not just a conceptual prototype such as we have in the literary delineation of the seven-panelled day of creation in the Genesis record, God's Sabbath is rather the original reality which was to confront mankind afterwards as a revelation of him who is to come in a judicial consummation of history, the reality encountered in redemptive history in the *parousia* of the Spirit-Lord,[55] the fulfillment of the biblical prophecies of the coming of the day of the Lord. As the imitative sign of this original day of the Lord, the human Sabbath ordinance is then not only a symbolic celebration of the lordship of God, the Alpha-

---

54. Cf., e.g., Revelation 1:8.
55. Cf. Revelation 1:7 and 8.

Creator, but a prophetic sign of the day of the Lord as a revelation of God, the Omega, in his eschatological coming for judgment.[56]

In connection with redemptive history, the judgmental function of the Lord's Sabbath includes prominently the aspect of victory over the enemy as prelude to the peace and rest of God's kingdom. This aspect is reflected in the development of the symbolism of the Sabbath sign. For example, God's judgment of the Canaanites is prerequisite to his establishment of Israel in the symbolic Sabbath-realm.[57] Similarly, in the Jubilee intensification of the Sabbath symbol, the great day of the Spirit is envisaged as a day of the vengeance of our God and thereby a day of liberation and restoration for the meek.[58] Even a meditation on the creation week is affected by this redemptive outlook: Psalm 104, having made its doxological way through the six days to the celebration of the Sabbath (vv. 31ff.), injects into the praise of the Lord's glory the prayer that the wicked be forever consumed from the earth (v. 35). In a related but more complicated phenomenon, prophecies of the redemptive Sabbath poetically appropriate the deep and the darkness—which in Genesis 1 are not, of course, personal-moral entities—as images of the powers of evil whom the Lord vanquishes on the great day.[59] Thus again, if only formally, the *yôm* of the Genesis Prologue is seen to have been a preformation of the eschatological day of the Lord.

Taking the pictorial prototype of the day of the Lord provided in the Genesis Prologue as a whole, sabbatical seventh panel and all, we see that it includes all the most significant aspects of that day— theological, spatial-cosmological, temporal-eschatological. It is a day of divine action featuring divine judgment with the penetration of the darkness by the light of theophanic Glory, it is a day of creating heaven

---

56. The garden-sanctuary in Eden represented the Glory as temple-kingdom and the recurring Sabbath was instituted to represent the Glory as the Spirit of the seventh day. Together, Eden and Sabbath are the space-time coordinates of the symbolism of the eschatological metamorphosis of the kingdom of God into the Glory-dimension.

57. Cf. Hebrews 4:8.

58. Cf. Isaiah 61:1ff.

59. In the background of this biblical development is the use of the deep-and-darkness in mythological traditions to set forth a confused fusion of physical and ethical realities. The biblical usage involves demythologization of the pagan sources on the one hand and allegorical adaptation of certain elements in Genesis 1 on the other (which is not to be confused with interpreting Genesis 1 allegorically).

and earth and consummating a temple of God made in the likeness of the Glory, it is a day of the revelation of the sovereign glory of the covenant Lord. Taken together, the seven days are the fulness of time of creation, the sevenfold fulness of the day of the Lord. In redemptive re-creation, the day of the Lord, wherein the old passes away and all is created new, is again a fulness of time, in which, as Paul declares, all the mystery of God comes finally into eschatological realization.[60] Standing between Moses and Paul, Isaiah links the creation and re-creation concepts of the day of the Lord as a fulness of time. He prophesies that "in the day" of the Lord's saving action "the light of the sun will be sevenfold, as the light of seven days" (Isa. 30:26). The day of the Spirit, both Alpha and Omega, is a sevenfold fulness of time, a manifestation of the full mystery of the sevenfold glory of the Spirit.[61]

It is this great and notable day of the Lord as presented in prototype in the day of the Spirit in the Genesis Prologue that is in view, illuminating and illumined, when Genesis 3:8 refers to "the Spirit of the day." When man broke the covenant, the Lord came as the Spirit of judicial light, as the *parousia*-Presence bringing the day of the Spirit.

The Primal *Parousia* and the Old Testament

Prophecies of the redemptive day of the Lord are cast in the mold of the primal *parousia* of Genesis 3:8. In putting it this way we do not mean to say that this is just a matter of conceptual stereotyping in a literary tradition.[62] There are actual objective historical realities in

---

60. See Galatians 4:4; Ephesians 1:9f.; cf. Matthew 13:11ff.; Mark 1:15; Colossians 1:15–20; Revelation 10:7.
61. See Revelation 4:5,11; 5:6; cf. 1:14.
62. Form-critical and traditio-historical analyses have led to various suggestions as to the source of the *yôm yhwh:* eschatology influenced by mythological notions of cyclic cosmic catastrophe and renewal, festival days of the deity in the cult, holy war traditions of God's day of battle, judgment days of the covenant lawsuit—or some combination of these. What, if any, historical factuality might lie behind these traditions is usually left discreetly obscure in studies conducted along these lines. But the *yôm yhwh* is not just an idea whose emergence is to be explained as derivative from one or more traditions found in biblical literature; it is an antecedent historical reality. And the reason that the day of the Lord is in evidence in such a variety of major biblical

view which are identical.[63] Of course, the literary rendering of the historical reality has its own existence with its own continuities of word and image, and this too is part of what we are concerned with—it is indeed the immediate data we are dealing with—as we trace the connection between the Lord's *parousia* in Eden and subsequent *parousia*-events foretold in biblical prophecy. Only a brief suggestive sampling can be given here of a vast amount of relevant biblical data. Our interest is especially in Old Testament passages that are more distinctly allusive to Genesis 3:8 (and thus have particular value for establishing the exegesis of that passage as an original day of the Lord) and on the New Testament's representation of the *parousia* of our Lord Jesus (with the light that might be thrown forward on this as its several components are traced back through the Old Testament to Genesis 3:8).

The canonical collection of Old Testament prophets closes with Malachi's announcement of the coming of the day of the Lord (especially Mal. 3:1; 4:1, 5 [3:19, 23]). That day is foreseen as the time when God takes decisive action (3:17; 4:3 [3:21]), when the Lord approaches for the purpose of judgment ($l^e mišpāṭ;$ 3:5), to administer the covenant lawsuit (3:1, 5), judicially separating the righteous from the wicked (3:18).[64] It is the advent of the Judge which is here definitive of the day (3:1, 2; 4:6 [3:24]).[65]

For our study of the relation of the Glory-Spirit to the day, it is instructive to observe how the coming Lord and the day become interchangeable in Malachi and elsewhere. Attributes of the Lord are attributed to the day. Like the Lord, the day is called "great and dreadful" (Mal. 4:5 [3:23]).[66] Like the Lord, the day has its advent; it is said to

---

traditions is that the judicial theophanic Presence, which constitutes the heart of the *yôm yhwh*, was a dominant reality, sovereignly active throughout the entirety of Israel's historical existence.

63. The identity affirmed allows for modal variations in the primal and later *parousia* events.

64. Cf. Malachi 2:17. The apostates blasphemously asserted that the Lord did not distinguish between good and evil. This is one of several possible indications in the terminology and ideas of the context just before Malachi 3 that the prophet's thoughts were ranging back to the garden and man's Fall.

65. According to Malachi 3:1, this advent is a coming of the Angel of the covenant, the divine figure peculiarly identified with the Glory-Spirit at the exodus.

66. See also Joel 2:11, 31 and Zephaniah 1:14. On the use of these terms to describe the Lord, see Psalms 76:1(2); 99:3; Daniel 9:4; Malachi 1:14.

be coming (Mal. 4:1, 5 [3:19, 23]). This "coming" is not that of bare chronological futurity but of visualized arrival;[67] specifically, it is here a dawning (Mal. 4:1, 2 [3:19, 20]). Since dawning is the way ordinary days come, the sunrise imagery would naturally arise once the advent idea was applied to the eschatological day. Nevertheless, this sunrise mode of the coming of the great day does match the Lord's *parousia*, which is visually a coming in radiant, earth-illuminating light.[68] Moreover, the dependence of this description of the dawning day of the Lord on the reality of the coming of the Glory of the Lord himself appears in the effects attributed to the day's dawning: it brings the light of judgment on the earth. This correspondence in judicial functioning of the Lord and the day extends to the dual nature of the judicial sanctions they carry out. The Glory-cloud was the agent of both the blessings and curses of the covenant. Thus, in the day of the exodus[69] the theophanic cloud provided guiding light and protective shade for Israel, but brought confusing darkness and destructive glare on the Egyptians.[70] Malachi pictures the light of the coming great day as similarly twofold in its effects, bringing the curse of burning and the blessing of healing (Mal. 4:1, 2 [3:19, 20]).[71]

That the judgment of the day is not to be construed narrowly in terms of condemnation and punishment is clear from the prototypal concep-

---

67. This arrival is sometimes described as near or hastening; cf. Ezekiel 7:7; 30:3; Joel 3:14; Obadiah 15; Zephaniah 1:14.

68. See Ezekiel 43:2. The figure of the wings (Mal. 4:2[3:20]) was probably suggested by the winged cherubim which are a prominent feature of the Glory and give rise elsewhere too to the use of the imagery of wings with reference to it (cf. pp. 14ff.). The symbol of the winged sun-disc as an emblem of divine majesty may be recalled here. Ultimately, Malachi's identification of the Lord's coming in Glory-light with the coming of the light of the great day must be traced to the connection of the Glory-Spirit with the dawning day-light of day one in Genesis 1, where the Spirit's identification as "Spirit of the day" begins to find its explanation.

69. For the use of "day" for this event, cf. Judges 19:30; I Samuel 8:8; II Samuel 7:6; Psalm 78:42; Isaiah 11:16; Jeremiah 7:22; 11:4,7; 31:32; 34:13; Hosea 2:15. The judgment of Egypt and deliverance of Israel, together with the covenant-creation event at Sinai, constitute a comprehensive day of the Lord. One aspect of the *parousia* of the Glory not connected with the day in the Malachi passage, the *qôl yhwh*, is strikingly related to the day of the Lord's advent at Sinai, especially in the Deuteronomy 4:10ff. account. On the depiction of the exodus event as a new creation, with particular allusion to Genesis 1:2, cf. pp. 14ff.

70. Cf. my *By Oath Consigned*, pp. 68f.

71. For a further allusion to Genesis 3 in this passage, compare the imagery of Malachi 4:3 (3:21) with that in Genesis 3:15.

tion of the day in the Genesis Prologue, where judicial pronouncement took the form of God's approval of his creation acts. Condemnation looms large as an aspect of the great day in postlapsarian history—already and dramatically in Genesis 3:8—but without cancelling out the positive aspects of the day, as the Malachi passage attests.[72] The day of judgment announced by the prophets is a day of both light and darkness, of creative restoration as well as desolating destruction, a day of realization of a Sabbath-consummation of the cosmos as well as of reversion to a chaotic deep-and-darkness.[73] Rebellious peoples and hypocrites who assume it will be a day of light must be warned that they will experience it as a day of gloom and thick darkness.[74] Suffering saints are promised that the day will come for them as brightness, dispelling their present darkness,[75] as a day of judicial vindication and deliverance.[76]

In Genesis 3:8 the coming of the Spirit of the day, or the day of the Spirit, was signalized by the voice *(qôl)* of the Lord. This distinctive identifying sound of the day of the Lord is very conspicuous in the account of the revelation of the Lord at Sinai in Deuteronomy 4:10ff.[77] As an example of this in the Prophets we may take the treatment of the day-of-the-Lord theme in Zephaniah. The expression "the sound *(qôl)* of the day of the Lord" appears in Zephaniah 1:14. It is the sound of a day of battle, of trumpet blast and warriors' shout (1:14, 16).[78] Reminiscence of Genesis 3 is suggested by certain contextual features: the *parousia* of the Lord on this day that is hastening near (1:7, 14; 2:2) with clouds and thick darkness (1:15) is for judicial purpose (3:8),[79] to

---

72. For a full and balanced presentation of the eternal curses and blessings introduced by the eschatological day, see Zechariah 14.

73. Cf., e.g., Isaiah 13:9ff.; 34:4, 8ff.

74. See especially Amos 5:18-20; cf. vv. 8, 9; cf. Isaiah 10:17; Jeremiah 13:16; Ezekiel 30:3. The expectation of the hypocrites, though not justified for themselves, does witness to the persistence in popular tradition of the idea of the primal relation between the day of the Spirit-Lord and the light, delineated in Genesis 1.

75. See, e.g., Isaiah 60:1-3; cf. 59:16ff.

76. See, e.g., Isaiah 34:8; cf. 35:4.

77. See note 69 above.

78. See also Isaiah 13:4-6, where the approach of the coming day is disclosed by the sound of the tumult of the armies of the Lord. Cf. Isaiah 30:30f.; Jeremiah 25:30, 33; Joel 2:11; 3:14, 16.

79. The judicial idea is present in *l'd* whether it is read "for a witness" or "from my throne."

expose by the divine searchlamps (1:12a) those who feel secure in their conceit that the Lord will not do good or evil (1:12b).[80]

There are passages in Isaiah of special interest for our theme, but these will be introduced in connection with an investigation of the *parousia*-sign of Christ in the following section of New Testament data. At this point we turn to the prophecy of Joel for one further illustration of the continuance of the Genesis 3:8 tradition in the Old Testament. Present in this prophecy, as in Genesis 3:8, are the Spirit-cloud of judgment, the day, and the sound of Yahweh. Most distinctive and calling for special comment is the treatment of the Glory-cloud in Joel 2.

Joel begins with the kind of warning to the wicked which we have observed in other prophets:[81] the day was coming, it was near, but it would be thick darkness, the heartening light of God's Glory being shrouded by threatening storm clouds (2:1, 2a). But Joel carries this reversal motif much further in a satirical parody of the concept of God's advent entertained by the unrepentant.[82] They smugly expected to be overclouded by protective hosts of winged cherubim, the glorious retinue of their heavenly King. The day of the Lord would bring them a cloud of winged creatures indeed! Taking his inspiration from the devastating judgment with which his prophecy opens (1:2ff.), Joel boldly portrays the angelic armies of the Glory as a cloud of locusts.[83]

Since the theophanic Glory is the essential core of the day of the Lord, mention of its advent is to be expected in such an extensive portrayal of that day, and various elements in the Joel 2 description are

---

80. Here too the judgment of the day is two-sided; it brings vindication to God's oppressed people (3:11ff.) and wrath on those who sin against the Lord (1:2ff., 17ff.; 3:8).

81. See note 74 above.

82. Of form-critical interest is an example of the reversal motif applied to things divine in the Ugaritic texts. In the Canaanite mythology, Baal, a god of blessing, has his "house" on the majestic heights, place of Utopian fertility and lavish banquet. And Mot, a god of the curse, has his house too, but it is the reverse of Baal's. At least, according to the customary reading of the key text (UT 51), Mot's house is in the depths, a place of miry desolation and loathesome diet—noble inheritance for a god, this estate in corruption!

83. The locust plague imagery, obvious enough in the description of the day of the Lord in Joel 2:1-11, is also explicit again in 2:20, 25. Another possible parody of the Glory is the symbol of the stork-winged women of Zechariah 5. Note a possible blend of the two in the locusts with women's hair in Revelation 9:8. Cf. also Isaiah 33:3, 4.

in fact found to be familiar features of the Glory theophany as depicted elsewhere. The description begins by drawing on the account of the descent of the theophanic Presence on Sinai. There is the blowing of the trumpets on the holy mountain and the darkness of the thick clouds about the consuming divine fire (2:1–3).[84] The sound of the army of judgment[85] is likened to chariots and their appearance to horses,[86] reminding us of the Glory, which is a chariot-throne whose sound is that of the winged creatures who bore it.[87] Like those cherubim of the Glory-chariot, the agents of judgment in Joel 2:7f. advance straight ahead, not turned aside by any obstacle or opposition (cf. Ezek. 1:9, 12; 10:22). Cosmic convulsions accompany the advance of this army (Joel 2:10; cf. 2:31), as they do the *parousia* of the Glory,[88] and before it is heard Yahweh's thunder-voice (2:11; cf. 3:14, 16), which from Genesis 3:8 onwards has heralded the approach of the Spirit in judgment. And in phraseology very similar to that employed by Malachi in his rhetorical question about the day of the *parousia* of the Angel of the Glory (Mal. 3:2), Joel asks who is able to sustain his judicial cause[89] in the judgment event of the great and fearful day which he is foretelling (2:11). The conclusion therefore seems warranted that Joel's locust cloud is a grotesque masque for the cherubim cloud of the Glory-Spirit of the day.[90]

---

84. Cf. Exodus 19:16ff.; Deuteronomy 4:11, 36. Note the reference to Exodus 34:6 in Joel 2:13.
85. On the army imagery, cf. II Samuel 5:24; Ezekiel 1:24.
86. Cf. II Kings 2:11; 6:17.
87. See the comments on Ezekiel's vision of the Glory above.
88. Cf., e.g., Psalms 18:7ff. (8ff.); 68:7f. (8f.); Zechariah 14:4ff.
89. Psalm 112:5b indicates the force of the verb *kwl* used by both Joel and Malachi: "(the righteous) will sustain (Pilpel of *kwl*) his words in judgment." In Malachi 3:2 and Joel 2:11 "day" serves as the equivalent of "his words in judgment" as the object of *kwl* (Pilpel in Malachi, Hiph'il in Joel). Parallel to *kwl* in Malachi 3:2 is '*md*, often used for standing in court (cf., e.g., Pss. 76:7f. [8f.]; 106:23; 109:6; 130:3; Isa. 3:13; 50:8; Zech. 3:1).
90. The adaptation of Joel 2 in Revelation 9 tends to confirm the interpretation of Joel 2 as a nonterrestrial phenomenon. There the locust army apparently represents a demonic host under the fallen star, Apollyon, angel of the bottomless pit, a counterpart to the hosts of Glory under the Angel of the covenant (cf. Joel 2:11 and Mal. 3:1). Compare also Paul's theme of the Satanic masquerade: Satan masquerades as an angel of the Presence-light and his false super-apostles pose as true apostles (II Cor. 11:13–15), while the career of his counter-Christ culminates in a *parousia* masquerade (II Thess. 2:8, 9).

We noted above that there is in Joel 2 the same combination of Glory-Spirit, the day, and the sound of Yahweh that we find in Genesis 3:8. Joel's likening of the effects of the judgment to the transformation of the garden of Eden into a wilderness (2:3) is another intimation that the prophet's eye was on the primal advent of the Spirit of the day (Gen. 3:8).

The Primal *Parousia* and the New Testament

The several features of God's *parousia* as the Spirit of the day that are met with in Genesis 3:8 reappear in the New Testament revelation of the advent of Jesus Christ in glory. Spirit, Glory, *pānîm* (Presence, literally Face) are terms used in the Old Testament for the mode of theophanic presence assumed in God's coming to judgment in the garden and elsewhere. Corresponding Greek terms are applied to the climactic *parousia*-event in the New Testament, the terms attaching themselves now to the person of the glorified Jesus, the Spirit-Lord. He incarnates the Glory theophany.[91]

The term *parousia* itself denotes primarily presence,[92] with the idea that the presence is realized by way of a coming as a secondary connotation. In II Corinthians 4:6 Christ is identified as the Face of God; it is from the face[93] of Jesus that the light of the divine Glory now shines, the face which in the transfiguration-*parousia*[94] shone like the sun.[95] In the extended treatment of the *parousia* theme in II Thessalonians, the presence of the Lord Jesus, revealed from heaven in flaming judgment, is referred to as his face *(prosōpon)*, with glory *(doxa)* as a synonymous parallel (1:9).[96]

When Christ's *parousia* is spoken of as a revelation in glory, as it is repeatedly, what is in view is the specific idea that Jesus is the embod-

---

91. See footnote 40 above.
92. Its antonym is *apousia,* "absence"; cf. Philippians 2:12. See also note 94 below.
93. Cf. Hebrew 9:24, where *prosōpon,* "face," is used in allusion to the Shekinah-Face in the holy of holies. It is used in the Septuagint for *pānîm.*
94. The revelation of the majesty of Jesus on the holy mount when the Glory of the theophanic cloud was replicated in him is called by Peter "the power and *parousia* of our Lord Jesus Christ" (II Peter 1:16–18).
95. Cf. too Revelation 10:1.
96. Cf. also Revelation 6:16; 20:11.

iment of the theophanic Glory of God revealed in the Old Testament. Jesus so identifies his *parousia*-Glory when he says the Son of Man will come in the glory of his Father (Matt. 16:27; Mark 8:38; Luke 9:26). [97] Of the same import is the fact that the major features of the Old Testament Glory-cloud phenomenon reappear in the delineation of the glory of Jesus' *parousia*. It is an advent-presence amid clouds and accompanied by the heavenly army of angels.[98] Power *(dunamis)* is a recurring aspect of Christ's *parousia*,[99] and this was a familiar epithet of the theophanic Glory, associated with the designation of the theophany as God's hand.[100] Jesus also identified his *parousia*-glory as a throne-glory[101] and so connected it with the paramount feature within the Glory-cloud—the throne of God.[102]

Like the primal judgment-advent of Genesis 3:8 and the approach of the Glory theophany elsewhere in the Old Testament, the *parousia* of Jesus has its heralding sound. The *qôl yhwh*, "voice of Yahweh," is heard again as the Lord comes with shout of command, voice of archangel, trumpet of God.[103] In Hebrews 12 the voice of God assumes special prominence among the phenomena of the Glory-*parousia*. Equivalency of the new covenant Presence-*parousia* to the Old Testament Glory in this respect is expressly indicated in this passage: the cosmos-shaking voice of the Lord as he speaks from heaven at the eschatological judgment will answer to the terrifying, earth-shaking voice of God in his ancient descent in the theophanic cloud with sound of trumpet and voice of words on Sinai (vv. 19, 25f.).

The same kind of relationship that is found in the Old Testament between the Spirit-Glory and the day, accounting for the phrase "the Spirit of the day" in Genesis 3:8, also obtains between the *parousia*

---

97. Cf. John 17:5,24; Acts 7:2, 55.

98. Matthew 16:27; 24:30f.; 25:31; Mark 8:38; 13:26f.; Luke 9:26. See too I Thessalonians 4:16, 17; II Thessalonians 1:7; cf. Acts 1:9–11.

99. Matthew 24:30; Mark 13:26; Luke 21:27; II Thessalonians 1:9 *(ischus);* cf. II Peter 1:16, with its conjunction of power and *parousia*.

100. Cf., e.g., Exodus 15:6; 32:11; Deuteronomy 4:37; 9:29.

101. Matthew 19:28; 25:31.

102. See pp. 17f. and 39ff.

103. I Thessalonians 4:16. See also I Corinthians 15:52; II Peter 3:10; cf. Exodus 19:16; Zechariah 9:14. The motif of the thundering noises and sound of trumpets runs through the eschatological drama of the Book of Revelation, occurring particularly in association with divine epiphany (cf., e.g., 1:10,15; 4:5; 8–11, especially 10:3 and 11:19).

and the day in the New Testament. Thus, the day is used as a metonym for the *parousia* of the Lord, so that an advent is attributed to it. In response to the scoffers' question about the promise of "his coming," Peter insists "the day of the Lord will come" (II Peter 3:10, cf. 4). He even uses the expression "the *parousia* of the day of God" (II Peter 3:12). Paul often refers to the *parousia* of Christ as "the day of Jesus Christ."[104] In I Corinthians 3:13 the metonymic usage by which the day rather than the Lord is said to be coming and to have a *parousia* is carried to the extent of predicating of the day the act of judicial declaration of which the real subject is the Lord. In this passage the day is also said to be revealed[105] in fire,[106] whereas elsewhere it is the Lord who is said to be revealed[107] and to be the consuming fire. Like the *parousia* (whether of the Spirit in the Old Testament or of Christ in the New Testament), the arrival of this "day of God" is proclaimed by "a great noise" (II Peter 3:10). And like the day of the Spirit in Genesis it is a day of creation as well as judgment (II Peter 3:12, 13).

While commenting on the overlapping relation of the concepts of *parousia* and day, we may mention a New Testament passage in which the Sabbath instituted in Genesis 2:3 as a sign of the day of the Spirit contributes to the symbolism of an apostle's ecstatic experience of the Glory-*parousia* reality. Describing the circumstances of his vision of Christ as the Glory theophany incarnate, John writes: "I was in the Spirit on the Lord's day and heard behind me a great voice" (Rev. 1:10), a voice as of trumpet or mighty waters (v. 15). Here is a striking reminiscence of the combination of features encountered in Genesis 3:8—the Spirit, the day, and the voice. And of course, there was the *parousia* of the Glory itself, with Christ present as Lord of the covenant to pronounce judgment on the works of his servants[108] in words replete with echoes of the scene in Eden and identified as what the Spirit says to the churches.[109]

As in the case of the Spirit of the day at the Fall of man, so the

104. I Corinthians 1:8, cf. v. 7; 5:5; II Corinthians 1:14; Philippians 1:6, 10; 2:16; II Thessalonians 2:2, cf. v. 1.
105. Thus, if "day" is indeed the subject of the verb *apokaluptō*.
106. Cf. Malachi 3:2; 4:1 (3:19).
107. Cf. Luke 17:30; II Thessalonians 1:7, 8.
108. Revelation 1:11. Cf. Revelation 2 and 3.
109. See Revelation 2:7, 11, etc. For a similar combination of the enthroned Glory, the Spirit, and the voice see Revelation 4:1ff.

parousia (or day) of Christ, with its purpose of exposing and sentencing the guilty, has as its effect a panic of terror manifested in frantic, futile attempts to hide from the eyes of the divine Presence.[110] According to New Testament teaching, the *parousia* of our Lord, like the Glory theophany described in the record of Israel's history and in Old Testament prophecies of the day of the Lord, brings vindication to the saints in the midst of cosmic cataclysm.[111] And like the prototypal day of the Spirit in the Genesis Prologue, the *parousia* of Christ entails creation of heaven and earth, and Sabbath consummation.[112]

In sum, these equivalencies in nature and function and in effects and consequences clearly show that the *parousia* of Jesus is the New Testament form of realization of that Old Testament Glory theophany beheld in primal *parousia* in Genesis 3:8. Of many possible ramifications of this theme it would be tempting, for one thing, to examine the relationship between the *parousia* and baptism concepts, a relationship that becomes obvious as soon as it is seen that, like baptism,[113] the *parousia* too is a matter of the messianic Spirit and fire.[114] Baptism is a sign of the *parousia* of the Spirit in judgment.[115] But passing by this sacramental earthly sign, we shall conclude this chapter by giving some special attention to an eschatological heavenly sign of the *parousia*, the sign of the Son of Man in heaven.

Messiah's *parousia*-sign was a subject of Old Testament prophecy. The same prophet who spoke beforehand of the identifying birth-sign

---

110. See, e.g., Revelation 6:16, 17. On v. 17b, cf. Malachi 3:2.
111. Matthew 24:29ff.; Mark 13:24f; Luke 21:11, 25f.; Hebrews 12:18ff.; II Peter 3:10–12; Revelation 6:12ff.; 20:11.
112. II Peter 3:13.
113. Cf. Matthew 3:11f.; Luke 3:16f.; cf. Mark 1:8.
114. The episode of Jesus' own baptism is on the trajectory of the *parousia* of the Glory-Spirit, which begins in Genesis 1:2 and 3:8 and continues through the exodus-event (cf. I Cor. 10:2, which parallels Christian baptism in water and Spirit to the Mosaic baptism in water and Glory-cloud) to the final *parousia*. Jesus' baptism involved the paradigmatic *parousia* features of the advent of the Spirit (in avian form, cf. John 1:32,33), the accompanying voice from heaven, and the pronouncing of judgment (of approbation) on God's Son. In the associated episode of the temptation of Jesus, the avenging Glory-cherubim of the Genesis 3 history of the first Adam have a counterpart in the ministering angels (Matt. 4:11; Mark 1:13).
115. Included is the judgment of approbation manifested in the perfecting of the Glory-image and cosmic re-creation.

of Immanuel (Isa. 7:14) prophesied of his Glory-sign too. It would seem, moreover, that these prophecies of Isaiah were to the fore among the Scriptures that were before the mind of our Lord when presenting the eschatological discourse in which he referred to "the sign *(sēmei-on)* of the Son of Man in heaven" (Matt. 24:30). What then do Isaiah's prophecies, taken together with our identification of Old Testament and New Testament *parousia* phenomena, tell us about the identity of the heavenly sign of the Son of Man?

We have quoted Isaiah 11:10 twice above and do so once more now because of its relation to Matthew 24:30. "In that day there shall be a root of Jesse who shall stand as a banner *(lᵉnēs)* for the peoples; the nations shall rally to him and his royal resting place shall be [the] Glory." Again in the following verses it is said that in that day, the day of eschatological restoration of the exiled remnant,[116] the Lord will "set up an ensign *(nēs)* for the nations and shall assemble the outcasts of Israel, and gather together the dispersed of Judah from the four corners of the earth" (v. 12). Messiah himself, enthroned in the Glory, is here viewed as the rallying banner of the final, universal assembly.[117]

Several times elsewhere Isaiah speaks of the Glory-Spirit as the banner. In Isaiah 31, the Lord's descent over Zion for the defense of Jerusalem is compared to birds in flight (vv. 4, 5),[118] and he is pictured as a flaming ensign *(nēs)* from which the enemy princes flee in panic (v. 9).[119]

In Isaiah 49, after a promise to give the Servant as a light, to whom those in darkness will come from afar (vv. 5-9), God further promises: "I will lift up mine hand[120] to the Gentiles and set up my standard *(nissî)* to the people" (v. 22a). As a result, the sons and daughters of Zion will be brought home from the lands of the Gentiles, as a prey rescued from the oppressors (vv. 22b-26). The hand-standard of verse

---

116. There is possibly a reference to the Glory-cloud in *yāḏô*, "his hand," in verse 11. On the use of *yāḏ* for military signals, see Joshua 8:19; Isaiah 13:2; and note 120 below. Cf. also II Samuel 18:18; I Chronicles 18:3.

117. Cf. John 12:32. On the Glory as a banner, see pp. 20, 40, and 45.

118. Cf. Deuteronomy 32:11 for the comparison of the Glory-cloud and a bird.

119. On the identification of the divine Glory-ensign as fire and furnace (Isa. 31:9b), cf. Genesis 15:17.

120. Note the parallelism of "hand" and "standard" here and see note 116 above.

22 and the Servant-light of verse 6 accomplish the same mission of worldwide ingathering and are to be identified, so that here, as in Isaiah 11, the messianic Servant is seen as himself the Glory-light-banner.

A similar picture appears in Isaiah 59. "When the enemy comes in like a flood, the Spirit of the Lord will lift up a standard against him" (v. 19b).[121] The image of the standard belongs here to a military scene that finds the Lord arrayed as the divine warrior, bringing vengeance on his enemies (vv. 17, 18).[122] According to verse 19a, the standard raised by the Spirit (v. 19b) is the theophanic cloud (the Spirit himself), for it is denoted "the Name" and "the Glory." The use of the Name designation of the theophanic cloud is apt in a context where it is depicted as a standard, for such a military banner in Israel would be inscribed with God's name.[123] Here again the figure of the messianic Redeemer is brought into conjunction with the Glory-standard (v. 20). And the effect of the raising of the Glory-sign is again to inspire the fear of God from east to west (v. 19a). The banner will be a radiant gathering point, drawing Zion's far-off sons and daughters from among the Gentiles (Isa. 60:1ff.).

Once more in Isaiah 66 the same theme and imagery occur. The sound of the Lord will be heard executing vengeance (v. 6). This manifestation of God's wrath will be a revelation of his "hand" (v. 14).[124] The Lord will come with fire and whirlwind-like chariots (v. 15) for judicial proceedings with mankind (v. 16) and will set up a standard ('ôṯ)[125] against the idolaters (v. 19). That the standard is the

---

121. The verb, nôsᵉsāh, is best taken as a denominative of nēs. Cf. Psalm 60:4(6), where the verb and the noun are paired in poetic parallelism.
122. See p. 47 on the relation of the divine armor and Glory.
123. See Psalm 20:5(6); Isaiah 62:10, 12; (cf. Isa. 30:27, 28). See Y. Yadin, *The Scroll of the War of the Sons of Light against the Sons of Darkness* (London: Oxford U. Press, 1962), pp. 38ff. Iconographic and literary evidence from Mesopotamia reveals the use of military standards emblematic of divine presence. They are depicted in chariots receiving cultic veneration. They are also stationed at temple entrances. See Thomas W. Mann, *Divine Presence and Guidance in Israelite Traditions* (Baltimore: The Johns Hopkins University Press, 1977), pp. 74ff. and 265ff.
124. See notes 116 and 120 above.
125. On the use of 'ôṯ for the standard, see Numbers 2:2; cf. Isaiah 19:1, 19f. In the Qumran War Scroll, 'ôṯ is regularly used for the military banner; nēs and yāḏ are also used for signs.

Glory is evident, for the result of setting it up is that men of all nations see God's Glory (vv. 18b, 19b). Connected with this again is the gathering of the Lord's people out of the nations (v. 20). There is also a picture of the blessings of re-creation (vv. 22, 23)[126] and the cursed fate of God's enemies, who are portrayed as carcasses in a perpetual Gehenna (v. 24).[127]

Before relating these prophecies of the Glory-ensign to Matthew 24:30 we may note their use of the term "Spirit" for the Glory[128] and mention certain *parousia* passages in the New Testament which hark back to them and reflect this usage of "Spirit."[129]

Poetic parallelism characterizes the description of the Lord's judgment of the man of sin in II Thessalonians 2:8,[130] the brightness *(epiphaneia)* of his *parousia* being balanced by the "*pneuma* of his mouth." Beyond this stylistic intimation of an Old Testament orientation, there are indications in theme and terminology of a specific dependence on the Glory-ensign context of Isaiah 11. Messiah's destruction of all the wicked as he comes in judgment to save his people out of tribulation is the theme there too, and it is expressed by a parallelism in which "the rod of his mouth" is balanced by "the $rû^a h$ of his lips" (v. 4). Verse 2 had just observed that the $rû^a h$ of Yahweh, the Spirit who qualifies for judgment, rested on Messiah.[131] Then Messiah's appearance as the Glory-Spirit-ensign is pictured (vv. 10ff.). This Isaianic background of II Thessalonians 2:8 suggests that the "*pneuma* of his mouth" is the Spirit of judgment, the Spirit of the day.[132] And this is supported by the parallelism of this *pneuma* within

126. Cf. Isaiah 65:17.
127. Cf. Isaiah 34:3, 15.
128. Isaiah 11:1ff., 10 and 59:19.
129. Isaiah's treatment of the eschatological Spirit should be considered in connection with the New Testament's identification of the eschatological-glorified state as a Spirit-state.
130. Cf. II Thessalonians 1:9. It has been observed that in apocalyptic passages New Testament authors have a tendency to fall into the style of the Old Testament prophets.
131. Cf. Isaiah 30:27, 28; 42:1ff. and Matthew 12:18ff.
132. The image-symbol, "Spirit of his mouth," might then be the same as was enacted by Jesus when he blew on his disciples the wind of his mouth, interpreting it as symbolic of the Holy Spirit (John 20:22). If the expression refers to the Lord's words (cf. Ps. 33:6), an identification of these words with the Spirit is understandable in terms of such teaching as John 6:63 and Matthew 10:20, particularly when read against the background of Isaiah 11:2ff. and 42:1ff.

II Thessalonians 2:8 with the *parousia-epiphaneia*. The identification
of the latter with the radiant Glory-Spirit theophany is supported by the
allusion to Isaiah 11:10 as well as by the use of the term *epiphaneia*
itself.[133]

Isaiah's prophecy of the suffering Servant on whom the Spirit rests
also lies behind the *parousia* passage in I Peter 4, where again the
Glory-revelation is called Spirit. Those who share in Christ's suffer-
ings have a joyful prospect awaiting them at the revelation *(apokalu-
psis)*[134] of his divine glory (v. 13). Indeed, on those who participate in
Messiah's anointing-name (vv. 14a, 16), "the Spirit of Glory and God
rests," as is preeminently true of the Spirit-anointed Servant himself.

Turning now to Matthew 24:30 and "the sign of the Son of Man in
heaven," it has already been observed that the Lord's account of his
coming in the Olivet discourse consists of a whole cluster of features
that serve to identify the *parousia* with the Glory-Spirit theophany of
the Old Testament. His advent is to be an epiphany in radiant clouds
amid the holy angels of God's throne, attended by a great noise and
cosmic cataclysm.[135] Now, "the sign of the Son of Man in heaven" (v.
30a) is nothing other than this epiphany itself. Accordingly, what the
tribes of the earth are said to see when the sign of the Son of Man
appears is "the Son of Man coming on the clouds of heaven with
power and great glory" (Matt. 24:30b). The Lord revealed as the
living embodiment of the Glory-Presence is himself the sign of the
parousia.[136]

At Jesus' birth, his identifying sign *(sēmeion)* was his clothing, the
swaddling clothes, the garment of his humiliation, and his position,
lying in the manger (Luke 2:12).[137] At his coming again, the identify-

---

133. Cf. I Timothy 6:14–16; II Timothy 4:1, 8; and especially Titus 2:13, which
speaks of the epiphany "of the glory of the great God."
134. On the noun, cf. I Corinthians 1:7; II Thessalonians 1:7; I Peter 1:7. On the verb
apokaluptō, cf. Luke 17:30; I Corinthians 3:13.
135. See above, notes 98, 99, 111.
136. Cf. Matthew 24:3. The phenomena in the heavens that accompany the Glory-
parousia are called "signs" in Luke 21:11, 25. The Glory is *the* sign; the luminaries
are reflective signs. This is in keeping with the status of the luminaries as replicas of
the Glory-Spirit, the archetypal light (cf. note 49 above), and with the function assigned them at creation (Gen. 1:14).
137. Cf. Ezekiel 16:4.

ing (name-)sign of his exaltation will be the Glory-robe in which he is
arrayed, his Spirit-clothing, and his position, standing in the heavens.
The shepherds were directed to find in the personal condition of the
infant Jesus himself, not in something apart from him, his name-sign.
So too the inquiring disciples were told that they would know Jesus in
his *parousia* by the glory of his own person, as he comes invested with
the name above every name.[138] The *parousia*-Glory is a self-
identifying, self-authenticating signature of God.

In his eschatological discourse our Lord was clearly drawing upon
Isaiah's prophecies of the *parousia*-sign. That Jesus, in his word about
the sign of the Son of Man in heaven, was introducing anew Isaiah's
theme of the Glory-ensign is put beyond question by the fact that the
sign in each case performs the same distinctive function. The function
of the Glory-ensign in Isaiah's prophecies—and the importance of the
matter is evident in that every one of the relevant passages mentions
it—is the gathering of God's people from the ends of the earth. In
Matthew 24, immediately after the reference to the Glory-sign itself,
comes the statement that the Son of Man will send his angels with the
sound of trumpet to gather the elect from one end of heaven to the other
(Matt. 24:31; Mark 13:27). And if Jesus' words at this point are clearly
in direct continuity with Isaiah's prophecies of the Glory-ensign,[139] the
interpretation of the sign of the Son of Man which sees it as the
apocalypse of the Messiah as the Glory-Spirit is confirmed.

More than that, the Isaianic prophecies indicate that the particular
imagery in view in "the sign of the Son of Man in heaven" is that of

---

138. The announcement of the birth-sign came through a revelation of the Glory of the
Lord of angelic hosts, so that the Glory-sign of the *parousia* served as a sign of the first
advent too. And as the stars of heaven, replicas of the Glory, are ancillary signs of the
parousia, so they too functioned at the first advent as an accompanying sign of the one
born king of the Jews (Matt. 2:2).
139. Further evidence of this is found in the relation that can be traced between the
saying about the eagles and the carcass conjoined to Jesus' prophecy of his coming
(Matt. 24:28) and the statement about the carcasses of the wicked in the final Glory-
ensign prophecy of Isaiah (66:24). The two passages are interlinked by Isaiah 34. The
phraseology of the prediction about the birds of prey in Isaiah 34:15 and the statement
in Isaiah 34:3 about the carcasses of the victims of God's vengeance are utilized in
Matthew 24:28. Isaiah 34:3 is also echoed in Isaiah 66:24 (this being but one detail in a
broad similarity between Isaiah 34 and 35, the close of the first part of the work, and
Isaiah 66, which closes the second part).

the military standard (called *nēs* or '*ōṯ* by Isaiah). The metaphorical depiction of the Glory-cloud as a military standard was natural; for on the one hand, these battle flags (as noted earlier)[140] were identifying name-banners and, on the other hand, the Glory-cloud as the revelation of God is in the biblical idiom sometimes called "the Name" of God. The military metaphor of the standard becomes quite explicit in the description of the *parousia* of the Word of God in Revelation 19:11ff. In this picture of Jesus as the incarnate Glory,[141] leading the armies of heaven to war, he is portrayed as a veritable living name-banner, inscribed on both Glory-robe and Spirit-body with the name that belongs to him alone (v. 12):[142] "King of kings and Lord of lords" (v. 16).[143]

The military image of the battle-standard fits readily into the Matthew 24 context, where its companion battle-signal, the trumpet,[144]

---

140. See note 123 above. For the Glory as Name, cf. p. 54.

141. Note the features in Revelation 19:12, 15 adopted from the vision of the Lord in Revelation 1:13ff.

142. Neither the extent of the influence of Old Testament *yāḏaʿ* on *oida* in the New Testament nor the precise meaning borne at times by *yāḏaʿ* has been sufficiently appreciated. The basic meaning of *yāḏaʿ*, "know," grades into "acknowledge, acknowledge as one's own, own." A close parallel to Revelation 19:12 is found in Zechariah 14:7, which also deals with the day of the Lord's *parousia,* declaring that it is acknowledged as the Lord's or belongs to the Lord (not, as usually rendered, "it is known to the Lord"). The recognition of this meaning for *oida* (viz., own as belonging to oneself) is recommended by and at the same time clarifies a passage like Matthew 7:23 (cf. Matt. 25:31ff.). That the idea in Revelation 19:12 is not that of the incomprehensibility of God (as, e.g., in Judg. 13:18) is evident from the use of the same idiom in Revelation 2:17 for the name received by the victorious saints. There too, the point is that none but the overcomers owns the name; the name belongs to no others. In Revelation 19, verses 15b and 16 answer questions raised by verses 12b and 13a. The arrangement is chiastic; verse 15b accounts for the blood on the warrior's robe (cf. v. 13a) and verse 16 informs us where the warrior's name was inscribed and what it was (cf. v. 12). This prophecy of the *parousia* Glory-banner is based on Isaiah 63:1ff., a passage where we find a particularly plain instance of *yāḏaʿ* in the sense of "own, acknowledge" (see Isa. 63:16). This passage could be added to the series of Glory-ensign prophecies in Isaiah cited above (cf. Isa. 62:10). In this connection the use of *proginōskō* in the sense of "own, claim for oneself, elect" (Rom. 8:29; 11:2; cf. I Peter 1:2) should also be mentioned.

143. Cf. Revelation 19:11, 13. Here again the theme of a universal gathering for judgment is immediately associated with that of the Glory-banner.

144. Cf. I Thessalonians 4:16. On the importance of the trumpet signals in the military practice of Israel and in the Qumran War Scroll, see Yadin, *The Scroll of the War of the Sons of Light against the Sons of Darkness,* pp. 87–113.

as well as the angel legions are also mentioned. The trumpet signal of Matthew 24:31 summons the people of God to their ranks in those heavenly armies[145] which are seen in Revelation 19:14 following the messianic warrior on the white horse to the final judgment.[146] And the Spirit-Lord whom they follow is his own battle-standard. The Son of Man in heaven is himself the sign, the name-banner, of the Son of Man. Invested with the Glory-Name, he comes in the day of the Lord as the Spirit of the day.

---

145. Cf. Numbers 10:9.
146. With Revelation 19:14 compare verse 8 and 3:4, 5; 6:11; 7:9, 13.

Index of Biblical References